This Book Belongs To

_ _

Start Planning Your Trip To Pennsylvania

Pennsylvania, the Keystone State, was one of the 13 original colonies of America.

It was named by King James II by combining the Latin word for "woodland", "Sylvania", and the surname of Admiral Sir William Penn.

It achieved statehood in 1787 and is a notable area to visit for history buffs thanks to its many significant roles in time.

It is here that the Declaration of Independence was signed and the Liberty Bell first tolled, and it is also home to sites that were central in the American Revolutionary War and American Civil War.

Naturally, all this history means that Pennsylvania is packed with exciting attractions.

From sprawling gardens to ornate feats of architecture and from historical buildings and museums to art galleries and institutes, there's no shortage of places that you can visit.

So, where to first?

To help you decide, here is our travel guide for 50 fun things to do and places to visit in Pennsylvania!

Happy Adventure.

YOUR FEEDBACK MEANS A LOT FOR US!

Please, Consider leaving us "5 stars" on your
Amazon review.
Thank You!

Copyright © 2022. Akeem Press. All Rights Reserved

No part of this book may be reproduced or transmitted in any form
or by any means, electronic or mechanical, including photocopying
recording or by any other form without written permission from
the publisher.

P	PLACES TO GO	LOCATION	EST.	VISITED
	EASTERN STATE PENITENTIARY	PHILADELPHIA	1829	
	ANDY WARHOL MUSEUM	PITTSBURGH	1994	
	FALLINGWATER	MILL RUN	1936	
	HERSHEYPARK	HERSHEY	1906	
	PENNSYLVANIA STATE CAPITOL COMPLEX	HARRISBURG	1906	
	GETTYSBURG NATIONAL MILITARY PARK	GETTYSBURG	1966	
	VALLEY FORGE NATIONAL HISTORIC PARK	KING OF PRUSSIA	1976	
	PHIPPS CONSERVATORY	PITTSBURGH	1893	
	PHILADELPHIA MUSEUM OF ART	PHILADELPHIA	1876	
)	RODIN MUSEUM	PHILADELPHIA	1929	
1	MOUNT MORIAH CEMETERY	PHILADELPHIA	1855	
2	INDEPENDENCE NATIONAL HISTORICAL PARK & THE LIBERTY BELL	PHILADELPHIA	1956	
3	PHILADELPHIA'S MAGIC GARDENS	PHILADELPHIA	2008	
4	CAVE OF KELPIUS	PHILADELPHIA	1694	
5	CARNEGIE MUSEUM OF NATURAL HISTORY	PITTSBURGH	1895	
6	SHOFUSO JAPANESE HOUSE AND GARDEN	PHILADELPHIA	1958	
7	MERCER MUSEUM AND FONTHILL CASTLE	DOYLESTOWN	1908	
8	DUTCH WONDERLAND	LANCASTER	1963	
9	THE SONOROUS STONES OF RINGING ROCKS PARK	UPPER BLACK EDDY	....	
)	PENN'S CAVE	CENTRE HALL	1885	
1	THE FRANKLIN INSTITUTE & THE FOUCAULT PENDULUM	PHILADELPHIA	1824	
2	LONGWOOD GARDENS	KENNETT SQUARE	1937	
3	WHARTON ESHERICK MUSEUM	MALVERN	1926	
4	PHILADELPHIA ZOO	PHILADELPHIA	1874	
5	THE BARNES FOUNDATION	PHILADELPHIA	1922	
6	STATE MUSEUM OF PENNSYLVANIA	HARRISBURG	1905	
7	INDIAN ECHO CAVERNS	HUMMELSTOWN	1929	
8	THE HERSHEY STORY	HERSHEY	1903	
9	SUSQUEHANNA ART MUSEUM	HARRISBURG	1903	
)	RAILROAD MUSEUM OF PENNSYLVANIA	STRASBURG	1975	
1	BRANDYWINE CONSERVANCY & MUSEUM OF ART	CHADDS FORD	1967	
2	LAKE TOBIAS WILDLIFE PARK	HALIFAX	1965	
3	CHANTICLEER	WAYNE	1913	
4	LACKAWANNA COAL MINE	SCRANTON	1860	
5	EDGAR ALLAN POE NATIONAL HISTORIC SITE	PHILADELPHIA	1843	
6	NATIONAL CIVIL WAR MUSEUM	HARRISBURG	2001	
7	WAGNER FREE INSTITUTE OF SCIENCE	PHILADELPHIA	1855	
8	FLIGHT 93 NATIONAL MEMORIAL	STOYSTOWN	2002	
9	KING OF PRUSSIA MALL	KING OF PRUSSIA	1963	
)	EISENHOWER NATIONAL HISTORIC SITE	GETTYSBURG	1980	
1	STEAMTOWN NATIONAL HISTORIC SITE	SCRANTON	1986	
2	PRESQUE ISLE STATE PARK	ERIE	1921	
3	ALLEGHENY PORTAGE RAILROAD	GALLITZIN	1834	
4	BLACK MOSHANNON STATE PARK	PHILIPSBURG	1937	
5	CALEDONIA STATE PARK	FAYETTEVILLE	1903	
6	CODORUS STATE PARK	HANOVER	1970	
7	DELAWARE WATER GAP NATIONAL RECREATION AREA	BUSHKILL	1965	
8	FRENCH CREEK STATE PARK	ELVERSON	1946	
9	FRIENDSHIP HILL HISTORIC SITE	POINT MARION	1789	
)	GIFFORD PINCHOT STATE PARK	LEWISBERRY	1961	

Inventory

☐ Binoculars	☐ Sport Shoes
☐ Bear Spray	☐ Swim Wear
☐ Cell Phone + Charger	☐ Towel
☐ Camera + Accessories	☐ Rainproof Backpack Cover
☐ First aid kit	☐ Pendrive
☐ Flashlight / Headlamp	☐ Powerbank
☐ Fleece / Waterproof Jacket	☐ Laptop
☐ Guide Book	☐ Small Tripod
☐ Hand Lotion	☐ Phone Holder
☐ Hiking Shoes	☐ Extender Cable
☐ Hand Sanitizer	☐ Bulbs / Fuses
☐ Insect Repellent	☐ Scissors
☐ Lip Balm	☐ Tent
☐ Medications & Painkillers	☐ Trash Bags
☐ Maps	☐ Umbrella
☐ Ticket / Pass	☐ National Park Maps
☐ Snacks	☐ National Park Maps
☐ Sunglasses	☐ Cosmetics
☐ Spare Socks	☐ Passport / Photocopy
☐ Sunscreen	☐ Id Card
☐ Sun Hat	☐ Driver's License
☐ Trash Bags	☐ ATM Cards
☐ Toilet Paper	☐ Cash
☐ Walking Stick	☐ Green Card
☐ Water	☐ Tool Box

Eastern State Penitentiary

VISTED DATE :   SPRING ◯ SUMMER ◯ FALL ◯ WINTER ◯

WEATHER : ☀◯ ⛅◯ 🌧◯ 🌨◯ ⛈◯ 🌬◯   🌡 TEMP :

FEE(S) :   RATING : ☆ ☆ ☆ ☆ ☆   WILL I RETURN? YES / NO

LODGING :   WHO I WENT WITH :

DESCRIPTION / THINGS TO DO :

THE EASTERN STATE PENITENTIARY IS AN EERIE STRUCTURE THAT RESEMBLES A CASTLE BUT HELD A VERY DIFFERENT PURPOSE. AN AMALGAMATION OF THE OLD AND THE NEW, IT IS A PRISON AND BOASTS STONE CONSTRUCTION, FORTRESS-LIKE ARCHWAYS AND CORRIDORS, INDUSTRIAL-STYLE SIMPLISTIC WATCHTOWERS, AND FORMERLY "HI-TECH" FIXINGS. IT WAS BUILT IN THE YEAR 1829 AND CLOSED IN 1971, AND AS OF ITS LAST DAYS, IT WAS ONE OF AMERICA'S LEADING FACILITIES OF ITS KIND. BEFORE THE CREATION OF THE EASTERN STATE PENITENTIARY, MOST PRISONS HAD ACTUALLY BEEN AKIN TO COMMERCIAL SPOTS. THERE WAS LITTLE ORDER IN THEM, WITH CORRUPT OFFICERS, PROSTITUTES, LOTS OF ALCOHOL, AND A HIGH RATE OF PRISONER DEATH BEFORE SENTENCING. THE EASTERN STATE PENITENTIARY WAS DESIGNED TO COMBAT THESE "TRENDS", MADE BY THE SOCIETY FOR ALLEVIATING THE MISERIES OF PUBLIC PRISONS. THE BUILDING WAS ONE OF THE WORLD'S MOST EXPENSIVE BUILDINGS IN ITS TIME, WITH AN $800,000 PRICE TAG. IN ITS DAY, THE EASTERN STATE PENITENTIARY WAS VERY MUCH A TECHNOLOGICAL MARVEL.

IT SOUNDED LIKE A PARADISE, BUT THAT WAS ONLY ON THE SURFACE. PRISONERS WERE NOT ALLOWED TO INTERACT WITH ANY OTHER PRISONERS OR SPEAK TO ANY GUARDS. THEY EXERCISED, ATE, AND READ THE ONLY ALLOWED BOOK – THE BIBLE – ALONE. GUARDS WORE SHOE COVERS TO KEEP THE ENTIRE COMPLEX INCREDIBLY QUIET, CREATING COMPLETE SILENCE AND SOLITUDE. THE HOPELESS SOLITARY CONFINEMENT OF THE EASTERN STATE PENITENTIARY WOULD DRIVE MANY OF ITS PRISONERS INSANE.

THE EASTERN STATE PENITENTIARY CLOSED DOWN IN 1971 & WAS NARROWLY SAVED FOR DESTRUCTION FOLLOWING YEARS OF ABANDONMENT. IT REOPENED IN 1994 AND HAS BECOME ONE OF PENNSYLVANIA'S FAMOUS LANDMARKS, PROVIDING TOURS TO INTERESTED VISITORS. WHETHER FOR THE HISTORICAL VALUE, PHOTOGRAPHY OPPORTUNITIES, OR MACABRE EXPLORATION, IT'S ONE OF THE THINGS TO DO IN PENNSYLVANIA YOU SHOULDN'T MISS.

ADDRESS: 2027 FAIRMOUNT AVE, PHILADELPHIA, PA 19130, UNITED STATES

PASSPORT STAMPS:

NOTES :

Andy Warhol Museum

VISTED DATE :   SPRING ◯   SUMMER ◯   FALL ◯   WINTER ◯

WEATHER :   ☀️◯   ⛅◯   🌧️◯   🌨️◯   ⛈️◯   💨◯   🌡️TEMP :

FEE(S) :   RATING :   ☆ ☆ ☆ ☆ ☆   WILL I RETURN?   YES / NO

LODGING :   WHO I WENT WITH :

DESCRIPTION / THINGS TO DO :

ANDY WARHOL, THE ONE-AND-ONLY FAMOUS ARTIST WHO WAS A PROMINENT INFLUENCE IN THE WORLD OF POP ART, WAS BORN IN PITTSBURGH, PENNSYLVANIA. THE ANDY WARHOL MUSEUM PAYS TRIBUTE TO HIS LONG AND ILLUSTRIOUS CAREER AND LIFE, SPANNING FROM HIS BIRTH TO HIS LATTER YEARS, UP UNTIL HIS PASSING IN 1987.

IT IS THE LARGEST IN THE COUNTRY THAT IS DEDICATED TO A SINGLE ARTIST. AT THE ANDY WARHOL MUSEUM, YOU'LL GAIN INSIGHT INTO THE ARTIST AND HIS MANY PIECES, INCLUDING FAMOUS WORKS LIKE TOMATO SOUP CANS AND HIS PORTRAITS OF ELVIS AND MARILYN.

EXHIBITS ARE DEDICATED TO HIS LIFE AND TIMES.

THE MUSEUM COVERS SEVEN FLOORS AND HOUSES A LARGE PERMANENT COLLECTION FEATURING HIS WORKS AND AN ARCHIVE PACKED WITH RELEVANT DOCUMENTS TO THE GREAT ARTIST. DON'T FORGET TO POP INTO THE FACTORY PORTION OF THE ANDY WARHOL MUSEUM.

HERE, YOU'LL GET TO LEARN AND TRY SOME OF WARHOL'S OWN PERSONAL TECHNIQUES FOR HIS ART. ART EDUCATORS LEAD THE WAY, ALLOWING YOU TO TRY MAKING ACETATE COLLAGES, SILK SCREENINGS, AND DRAWINGS WITH BLOTTED LINES.

FOR ART LOVERS AND CURIOUS TOURISTS ALIKE, THIS IS ONE OF PENNSYLVANIA'S TOP 10 HOTSPOTS.

ADDRESS: 117 SANDUSKY ST, PITTSBURGH, PA 15212, UNITED STATES

PASSPORT STAMPS:

NOTES :

Fallingwater

VISTED DATE :   SPRING ◯ SUMMER ◯ FALL ◯ WINTER ◯

WEATHER : ☀◯ ⛅◯ 🌧◯ 🌨◯ ⛈◯ 🌬◯   🌡TEMP :

FEE(S) :   RATING : ☆ ☆ ☆ ☆ ☆   WILL I RETURN? YES / NO

LODGING :   WHO I WENT WITH :

DESCRIPTION / THINGS TO DO :

FALLINGWATER'S UNIQUE NAME IS A PRODUCT OF ITS ACTUAL APPEARANCE. KNOWN ALSO AS THE KAUF-
MANN RESIDENCE, IT IS CHIEFLY RECOGNIZED AS ONE OF THE FINEST PRIVATE HOMES DESIGNED BY THE
RENOWNED ARCHITECT FRANK LLOYD WRIGHT – AND ONE OF HIS BEST DESIGNS OVERALL! IT WAS BUILT
IN 1935 AND FEATURES A STRUCTURE THAT PROTRUDES OVER A WATERFALL IN PENNSYLVANIA'S FAYETTE
COUNTY, WHERE IT SITS ON BEAR RUN IN THE STEWARD TOWNSHIP AS ONE OF THE MOST LOVED PENNS-
YLVANIA ATTRACTIONS AND VACATION PLACES. FALLINGWATER COST $155,000 TO BUILD.

AS SOON AS IT WAS BUILT, FALLINGWATER WAS AN ARCHITECTURAL ICON AND WAS FEATURED IN MANY
PUBLICATIONS AND MAGAZINES. IN 1966, IT WAS DETERMINED A NATIONAL HISTORIC LANDMARK, AND
IN 1991, IT WAS CONSIDERED THE GREATEST WORK OF AMERICAN ARCHITECTURE BY THE AMERICAN INS-
TITUTE OF ARCHITECTURE.

THE HOME IS THE ONLY MAJOR WORK BY WRIGHT THAT IS OPEN FOR THE PUBLIC, AND IT BOASTS MANY
ORIGINAL FEATURES AND COMPONENTS. THE KAUFFMANS FILLED FALLINGWATER WITH ART PIECES AND
COLLECTIONS OF ARTIFACTS THAT REMAIN ON DISPLAY FOR VISITORS TILL NOW. FOLK CRAFTS, SCULPTUR-
ES, AND EVEN DESIGNER FURNITURE MAKE UP THE OVERALL AESTHETIC. YOU'LL FIND A CAST-IRON BUD-
DHA HEAD DATING AS FAR BACK AS 906, AN 8TH-CENTURY SCULPTURE OF PARVATI THE HINDU FERTILITY
GODDESS, A MADONNA FROM 1420 OF AUSTRIAN-BOHEMIAN STYLE, UNIQUE CERAMICS AND SCULPTUR-
ES, AND COLLECTIONS OF ART BY PICASSO AND DIEGO RIVERA.

WORKS FROM MEXICO, AFRICA, AND OTHER CULTURES ADORN THE HOUSE, PROVIDING MANY SIGHTS TO
SEE ON YOUR VISIT.

ADDRESS: 1491 MILL RUN RD, MILL RUN, PA 15464, UNITED STATES

PASSPORT STAMPS:

NOTES :

Hersheypark

VISTED DATE :   SPRING ◯ SUMMER ◯ FALL ◯ WINTER ◯

WEATHER :   ☀️◯ 🌤️◯ 🌧️◯ 🌨️◯ ⛈️◯ 🌬️◯   🌡️ TEMP :

FEE(S) :   RATING : ☆ ☆ ☆ ☆ ☆   WILL I RETURN? YES / NO

LODGING :   WHO I WENT WITH :

DESCRIPTION / THINGS TO DO :

HERSHEYPARK IS A FUN AMUSEMENT PARK PACKED WITH ACTIVITIES THAT WILL AMUSE PEOPLE OF ALL AGES.

IT IS LOCATED IN THE FAMOUS PENNSYLVANIA TOWN OF HERSHEY, WHICH, AS ITS NAME MAY SUGGEST, IS VERY CLOSELY RELATED TO THE POPULAR HERSHEY'S BRAND OF CHOCOLATE.

SPANNING 90 ACRES, HERSHEYPARK IS THE MAIN ATTRACTION OF THE TOWN.

IT WAS ORIGINALLY BUILT AS A RECREATIONAL SITE FOR WORKS OF HERSHEY'S IN 1906, BUT IT EVENTUALLY EXPANDED — AND CONTINUES TO EXPAND!

AMONG THE THINGS TO SEE AND DO IN HERSHEYPARK ARE A TRAIN, FERRIS WHEEL, CAROUSEL, ROLLER COASTERS, A WATER PARK, BUMPER CARS, A ZOO, AN OBSERVATION TOWER, MIDWAY GAMES, VIDEO ARCADES, AND AN AMPHITHEATER WITH LIVE ENTERTAINMENT ACTS.

THERE ARE OVER 70 TOTAL ATTRACTIONS HERE AS WELL AS RESTAURANTS CATERING TO PEOPLE OF ALL PREFERENCES.

FOR AN EXCITING DAY IN PENNSYLVANIA, YOU CAN'T GO WRONG WITH HERSHEYPARK!

ADDRESS: 100 HERSHEYPARK DR, HERSHEY, PA 17033, UNITED STATES

PASSPORT STAMPS:

NOTES:

Pennsylvania State Capitol Complex

VISTED DATE :   SPRING ◯ SUMMER ◯ FALL ◯ WINTER ◯

WEATHER : ☀️◯ ⛅◯ 🌧️◯ 🌨️◯ ⛈️◯ 💨◯   🌡️TEMP :

FEE(S) :   RATING : ☆ ☆ ☆ ☆ ☆   WILL I RETURN? YES / NO

LODGING :   WHO I WENT WITH :

DESCRIPTION / THINGS TO DO :

THE PENNSYLVANIA STATE CAPITOL COMPLEX IS A NATURAL CHOICE FOR WHAT TO DO IN THE STATE.

SPANNING 45 ACRES OF LAND, IT IS HOME TO MULTIPLE TOURIST DESTINATIONS WITHIN AS WELL AS SEVERAL ACTIVE GOVERNMENT BUILDINGS.

IT FEATURES A HUGE DOME STYLED AFTER THE CATHEDRAL OF ST. PETER IN ROME, WHICH WAS BUILT HERE IN 1906 AND RESTS ON TOP OF THE MAIN COMPLEX, WHERE IT WEIGHS 52 MILLION POUNDS.

THE PENNSYLVANIA STATE CAPITOL COMPLEX'S MAIN BUILDING IS MADE FROM VERMONT GRANITE AND FEATURES A HUGE PART OF BRONZE DOUBLE DOORS.

TOURS INSIDE ARE AVAILABLE BUT HAVE TO BE PRE-SCHEDULED.

THE GORGEOUS ARCHITECTURE OF THE WHOLE AREA IS WORTH SEEING AND EXPLORING.

AND THE GROUNDS HOUSE MANY MEMORIALS AND MUSEUMS, INCLUDING THE STATE'S WAR VETERANS MEMORIAL FOUNTAIN AND THE SOLDIER'S GROVE QUADRANGLE.

ADDRESS: 501 N 3RD ST, HARRISBURG, PA 17120, UNITED STATES

PASSPORT STAMPS:

NOTES :

Gettysburg National Military Park

VISTED DATE :   SPRING ◯ SUMMER ◯ FALL ◯ WINTER ◯

WEATHER :   ☀️◯ ⛅◯ ☁️◯ 🌨️◯ ⛈️◯ 🌬️◯   🌡️TEMP :

FEE(S) :   RATING : ☆ ☆ ☆ ☆ ☆   WILL I RETURN? YES / NO

LODGING :   WHO I WENT WITH :

DESCRIPTION / THINGS TO DO :

THE GETTYSBURG NATIONAL MILITARY PARK IN PENNSYLVANIA IS THE SITE WHERE, IN 1863, THE AMERICAN CIVIL WAR'S BATTLE OF GETTYSBURG TOOK PLACE, TAKING 51,000 LIVES APPROXIMATELY IN ITS THREE-DAY RAGE.

TODAY, IT IS ADAMANT THAT VISITORS NEVER FORGET THOSE LIVES.

WITH MONUMENTS AND MARKERS THROUGHOUT THE LOCATION, TOTALING HUNDREDS, TO PROVIDE EDUCATIONAL INFORMATION TO GUESTS.

AMONG THE BEST SPOTS TO CHECK OUT AT THE GETTYSBURG NATIONAL MILITARY PARK ARE CEMETERY RIDGE, WHERE UNION LINES STOOD ON THE LAST TWO DAYS, OAK RIDGE, WHICH IS WHERE THE FIRST DAY'S BATTLE OCCURRED, AND SEMINARY RIDGE, WHERE CONFEDERATE LINES STOOD ON THE LAST TWO DAYS.

YOU CAN ALSO HEAD TO THE PARK MUSEUM AND VISITOR CENTER, WHERE YOU CAN VIEW ONE OF AMERICA'S LARGEST COLLECTION OF CIVIL WAR WEAPONS, UNIFORMS, AND PERSONAL ITEMS IN THE ROSENSTEEL COLLECTION.

THERE ARE ALSO PROGRAMS, EVENTS, HORSEBACK TRAILS, AND REENACTMENTS THAT MAKE THIS ONE OF THE MOST INTERESTING PLACES TO VISIT IN PA FOR HISTORY LOVERS.

ADDRESS: 1195 BALTIMORE PIKE, GETTYSBURG, PA 17325, UNITED STATES

PASSPORT STAMPS:

NOTES :

Valley Forge National Historic Park

VISTED DATE :   SPRING ◯   SUMMER ◯   FALL ◯   WINTER ◯

WEATHER :   ☀️◯   🌤️◯   🌧️◯   🌨️◯   ⛈️◯   🌬️◯   🌡️ TEMP :

FEE(S) :   RATING : ☆ ☆ ☆ ☆ ☆   WILL I RETURN?   YES / NO

LODGING :   WHO I WENT WITH :

DESCRIPTION / THINGS TO DO :

VALLEY FORGE NATIONAL HISTORIC PARK OF PENNSYLVANIA ARE A SYMBOL OF THE SACRIFICES, SUCCESSES, SUFFERING, AND ULTIMATE VICTORY OF THE AMERICAN REVOLUTIONARY WAR.

IT IS HERE THAT THE CONTINENTAL ARMY BUNDLED UP FOR THE WINTER OF 1777 TO 1778, WHERE THEY LIVED IN CRUDE CABINS MADE OF LOGS AFTER BRITISH TROOPS DESTROYED THEIR CENTER FOR SUPPLIES.

SOLDIERS HERE WERE CASUALTIES, WITH 2,000 OR SO OF THEM STRUGGLING FROM POOR CONDITIONS, HUNGER, AND DISEASE.

DESPITE THE WIND CHILLS, THEY LIVED, RESTED, AND TRIED TO SURVIVE FROM DECEMBER TO JUNE.

GEORGE WASHINGTON'S OWN HOUSE REMAINS HERE, AVAILABLE TO TOUR, A REMINISCENT GLIMPSE INTO THE PAST.

THE VALLEY FORGE NATIONAL HISTORIC PARK SPANS 3,500 ACRES AND BOASTS MULTIPLE TOURS, A NATIONAL MEMORIAL ARCH, PLENTY OF RECREATIONAL TRAILS AND SPACES.

AND FACILITIES LIKE RESTROOMS AND A CANTEEN.

FOR LOCALS AND TOURISTS ALIKE, EXPLORING AND SIGHTSEEING HERE IS ONE OF THE LOVELY THINGS TO DO IN PA.

ADDRESS: 1400 N OUTER LINE DR, KING OF PRUSSIA, PA 19406, UNITED STATES

PASSPORT STAMPS:

NOTES :

Phipps Conservatory

VISTED DATE :   SPRING ◯ SUMMER ◯ FALL ◯ WINTER ◯

WEATHER : ☀◯ ⛅◯ 🌧◯ 🌨◯ ⛈◯ 🌬◯   🌡TEMP :

FEE(S) :   RATING : ☆ ☆ ☆ ☆ ☆   WILL I RETURN?   YES / NO

LODGING :   WHO I WENT WITH :

DESCRIPTION / THINGS TO DO :

PHIPPS CONSERVATORY IS A LARGE COMPLEX IN SCHENLEY PARK OF PITTSBURGH, PENNSYLVANIA.

IT SPANS 15 ACRES AND IS A PART OF THE NATIONAL REGISTER OF HISTORIC PLACES, WITH 14 ROOMS WITHIN THE MAIN CONSERVATORY BUILDING.

THE SPACE WAS DONATED TO PITTSBURGH IN 1893 BY HENRY PHIPPS, A REAL ESTATE AND STEEL MAGNATE WHO BUILT IT AS A PRESENT FOR THE CITY.

THE PHIPPS CONSERVATORY'S MAIN GOAL IS TO EDUCATE GUESTS AND PROVIDE A FUN EXPERIENCE FOR ALL VISITORS.

IT BOASTS 23 GARDENS SUCH AS THE ROOFTOP EDIBLE GARDEN, CHILDREN'S GARDEN, AND JAPANESE GARDEN, A CENTER FOR SUSTAINABLE LANDSCAPES, AND OF COURSE, THE CONSERVATORY GLASSHOUSE, MADE IN A VICTORIAN STYLE.

THE 14 ROOMS OF THE PHIPPS CONSERVATORY GLASSHOUSE ARE PACKED WITH ALL SORTS OF EXOTIC PLANTS.

THIS INCLUDES SPICES, ORCHIDS, PALM TREES, TROPICAL FRUITS, FERNS, BONSAI, AND EVEN A DESERT ROOM BOASTING CACTI AND A TROPICAL FOREST CONSERVATORY THAT FEELS LIKE IT'S A WORLD AWAY FROM THE STATE. THEMED FLOWER SHOWS, SPECIAL EVENTS, AND A BEAUTIFUL CHANDELIER ALL ADD TO THE EXPERIENCE, MAKING THIS ONE OF THE CHIEF PLACES TO VISIT IN PENNSYLVANIA FOR NATURE-LOVERS!

ADDRESS: 1 SCHENLEY DRIVE, PITTSBURGH, PA 15213, UNITED STATES

PASSPORT STAMPS:

NOTES :

Philadelphia Museum of Art

VISTED DATE :   SPRING ◯ SUMMER ◯ FALL ◯ WINTER ◯

WEATHER :   ☀◯ ⛅◯ 🌧◯ 🌨◯ ⛈◯ 💨◯   🌡TEMP :

FEE(S) :   RATING : ☆ ☆ ☆ ☆ ☆   WILL I RETURN?   YES / NO

LODGING :   WHO I WENT WITH :

DESCRIPTION / THINGS TO DO :

THE PHILADELPHIA MUSEUM OF ART IS HOME TO ONE OF THE COUNTRY'S BEST AND BIGGEST ART COLLECTIONS, AND IT'S ALSO ICONIC IN PENNSYLVANIA THANKS TO ITS FRONT STEPS' FEATURE IN THE ROCKY MOVIES.

MORE THAN 227,000 PIECES OF ART REST HERE, FROM AMERICAN TO EUROPEAN TO ASIAN ART, MAKING IT ONE OF THE WORLD'S MOST IMPORTANT ARTISTIC INSTITUTIONS.

PERMANENT COLLECTIONS AT THE PHILADELPHIA MUSEUM OF ART INCLUDE VERY VARIED WORKS OF ART, INCLUDING COSTUMES, ASIAN CERAMICS, DECORATIVE ARTS, AMERICAN COLONIAL FURNITURE, PAINTINGS, PHOTOGRAPHS, FASHION, PRINTS, ARMOR, DRAWINGS, TEXTILES, AND A SCULPTURE GARDEN OUTDOORS.

GREAT ARTISTS SUCH AS CÉZANNE, DALI, CHAGALL, PICASSO, REMBRANDT, MONET, MANET, RENOIR, VAN GOGH, AND MATISSE HAVE WORKS HERE.

AS ONE OF PENNSYLVANIA'S MOST ATTRACTIVE POINTS OF INTEREST FOR ART AFICIONADOS, YOU'LL BE PLEASED TO KNOW THAT THE PHILADELPHIA MUSEUM OF ART FEATURES WORK FROM THE TIMES OF FRENCH IMPRESSIONISM, THE RENAISSANCE, THE MIDDLE AGES, AND EVEN THE PRESENT DAY.

DON'T MISS A TRIP HERE IF YOU CAN HELP IT!

ADDRESS: 2600 BENJAMIN FRANKLIN PKWY, PHILADELPHIA, PA 19130, UNITED STATES

PASSPORT STAMPS:

NOTES :

Rodin Museum

VISTED DATE : SPRING ◯ SUMMER ◯ FALL ◯ WINTER ◯

WEATHER : ☀ ◯ ⛅ ◯ 🌧 ◯ 🌨 ◯ ⛈ ◯ 🌬 ◯ 🌡 TEMP :

FEE(S) : RATING : ☆ ☆ ☆ ☆ ☆ WILL I RETURN? YES / NO

LODGING : WHO I WENT WITH :

DESCRIPTION / THINGS TO DO :

THE RODIN MUSEUM SITS BETWEEN TWO PRESTIGIOUS BUILDINGS: THE FREE LIBRARY OF PHILADELPHIA AND THE AFOREMENTIONED PHILADELPHIA MUSEUM OF ART, YET ANOTHER ONE OF THIS PENNSYLVANIA CITY'S TOURIST PLACES.

IT IS MUCH MORE SPECIFIC THAN THE LARGER MUSEUM OF ART, FOCUSED ONLY ON THE EXHIBITION OF THE WORKS OF SCULPTOR AUGUSTE RODIN.

OPENED IN 1929, IT IS THE BIGGEST COLLECTION OF HIS WORKS OUTSIDE OF PARIS AND WAS A GIFT FROM A PHILANTHROPIST NAMED JULES MASTBAUM.

THE RODIN MUSEUM IS A BEAUTIFULLY DESIGNED BUILDING IN THE BEAUX-ARTS STYLE, FRINGED ALL AROUND BY FORMAL FRENCH GARDENS THAT HOLD MORE FUN AND INSIGHTFUL SCULPTURES BY RODIN.

THE SCULPTURE RIGHT OUTSIDE OF THE MUSEUM IS THE INCREDIBLY FAMOUS WORK, THE THINKER, AND VISITING TO SEE THAT IN ITSELF IS ONE OF THE THINGS TO DO IN PENNSYLVANIA.

INSIDE THE RODIN MUSEUM, CLOSE TO 150 DIFFERENT SCULPTURES REPRESENTING MANY DIFFERENT POINTS OF RODIN'S LIFE AND CAREER ARE ON DISPLAY.

THIS INCLUDES BRONZES, PLASTERS, MARBLES, PRINTS, AND EVEN WORKS IN PROGRESS. THE MUSEUM IS MANAGED BY THE PHILADELPHIA MUSEUM OF ART AND IS A MUST-SEE FOR FANS AND CURIOUS TOURISTS ALIKE.

ADDRESS: 2151 BENJAMIN FRANKLIN PKWY, PHILADELPHIA, PA 19130, UNITED STATES

PASSPORT STAMPS:

NOTES :

Mount Moriah Cemetery

DESCRIPTION / THINGS TO DO :

MOUNT MORIAH CEMETERY HAS A LONG HISTORY AND WAS ALMOST A FORGOTTEN, DESTROYED PORTION OF PENNSYLVANIA, BUT FOLLOWING SOME RESCUING.

IT HAS BECOME ONE OF SOUTHWEST PHILADELPHIA'S BEST UNUSUAL SPOTS FOR SIGHTSEEING.

THE CEMETERY ORIGINALLY OPENED IN 1855, BOASTING GOTHIC MAUSOLEUMS, A REGAL AND ORNATE ENTRANCE IN A ROMANESQUE BRICK STYLE, AND AN EVENTUAL EXPANSION OF 400 ACRES OF LAND TO BECOME THE BIGGEST BURIAL SITE IN PENNSYLVANIA.

INTERESTINGLY, NO ONE ACTUALLY OWNS THE CEMETERY, WHICH IS PART OF WHY IT BECAME ABANDONED AND FORGOTTEN.

FOR A TIME, IT SEEMED THAT MOUNT MORIAH CEMETERY WOULD SIMPLY BE RECLAIMED BY NATURE, AS THE HEADSTONES AND MONUMENTS WITHIN FELL AND OVERGROWTH OVERTOOK EVEN THE WEALTHIEST VICTORIAN GRAVES.

THAT'S WHEN THE FRIENDS OF MOUNT MORIAH, A LOCAL NON-PROFIT GROUP, STEPPED IN TO HELP.

WITH YEARS OF WORK, MORE THAN HALF OF THE CEMETERY HAS BEEN CLEARED UP AND IS REOPENED FOR EAGER EYES AND FUN, IF SOBERING, EXPLORATION.

ADDRESS: 6201 KINGSESSING AVE, PHILADELPHIA, PA 19142, UNITED STATES

PASSPORT STAMPS:

NOTES :

Independence National Historical Park and the Liberty Bell

VISTED DATE :   SPRING ◯ SUMMER ◯ FALL ◯ WINTER ◯

WEATHER : ☀️◯ 🌤️◯ 🌧️◯ 🌨️◯ ⛈️◯ 🌬️◯   🌡️TEMP :

FEE(S) :   RATING : ☆ ☆ ☆ ☆ ☆   WILL I RETURN?   YES / NO

LODGING :   WHO I WENT WITH :

DESCRIPTION / THINGS TO DO :

ONE OF THE BIGGEST AND MOST KNOWN PENNSYLVANIA ATTRACTIONS IS PROBABLY INDEPENDENCE NATIONAL HISTORICAL PARK AND ITS ACCOMPANYING LIBERTY BELL.

AN INCREDIBLY HISTORIC LOCATION, IT IS HERE IN THE PARK THAT THE DECLARATION OF INDEPENDENCE WAS SIGNED, AND THE TABLE THAT GEORGE WASHINGTON USED IS STILL ON-SITE FOR VISITORS TO OGLE.

IT IS ALSO A WORLD HERITAGE SITE.

THE CENTRAL FEATURE OF INDEPENDENCE NATIONAL HISTORICAL PARK IS INDEPENDENCE HALL, A GEORGIAN BUILDING OF RED BRICK AVAILABLE FOR RANGER-LED TOURS.

THE STRUCTURE WAS PENNSYLVANIA'S FIRST LEGISLATIVE BUILDING AND WAS BUILT IN 1763.

ACROSS THE STREET, THE LIBERTY BELL CENTER AND ITS FAMOUS CRACK REST, TWO TONS IN WEIGHT, AFTER ITS RINGING IN 1776 TO CELEBRATE INDEPENDENCE.

BEYOND THERE, YOU'LL FIND INDEPENDENCE MALL, WHICH EXTENDS NORTH AND HAS SINCE 1948.

IT LAYS OUT TRAILS TO CARPENTER'S HALL, OLD CITY HALL, AND CONGRESS HALL, AMONG OTHER HISTORIC BUILDINGS LINING THE COBBLESTONE ROADS.

ADDRESS: PHILADELPHIA, PA 19106, UNITED STATES

PASSPORT STAMPS:

NOTES :

Philadelphia's Magic Gardens

VISTED DATE :   SPRING ◯   SUMMER ◯   FALL ◯   WINTER ◯

WEATHER :   ☀️◯   ⛅◯   🌧️◯   🌨️◯   ⛈️◯   🌬️◯   🌡️TEMP :

FEE(S) :   RATING : ☆ ☆ ☆ ☆ ☆   WILL I RETURN?   YES / NO

LODGING :   WHO I WENT WITH :

DESCRIPTION / THINGS TO DO :

IF YOU'RE CHOOSING THE BEST THINGS TO SEE IN THE STATE OF PENNSYLVANIA, YOU SIMPLY MUST TAKE IN THE STUNNING SITE SEEING OPPORTUNITY THAT IS PHILADELPHIA'S MAGIC GARDENS. THE GARDENS ARE A NONPROFIT GROUP, A FOLK ARK CENTER, AND A GALLERY FOR THE WORKS OF ISAIAH ZAGAR, A FAMOUS MOSAICIST, ON THE SITE OF HIS BIGGEST PUBLIC INSTALLATION OF ART. IN THE LATE 1960S, ZAGAR BEGAN FOCUSING HIS EFFORTS ON BEAUTIFYING THE NEIGHBORHOOD OF SOUTH STREET AFTER MOVING HERE WITH HIS WIFE.

THE COUPLE HELPED REVIVE THE AREA BY BUYING AND REFURBISHING BUILDINGS THAT WERE FALLING APART, USING VIBRANT MOSAICS TO COLOR THE WALLS AND BRING LIFE TO THEM. THE FIRST BUILDING THEY DID THIS WITH WAS THE EYES GALLERY, WHICH REMAINS OPEN AND DOING WELL NOW.

ZAGAR'S WORK ON THE MAGIC GARDENS BEGAN IN 1994, USING A VACANT LOT THAT WAS CLOSE TO HIS STUDIO. FOR 14 YEARS, HE EXCAVATED GROTTOS AND TUNNELS, SCULPTURED WALLS IN LAYERS, ADDED GROUTING AND TILING AND PERFECTED 3,000 SQUARE FEET OF SPACE.

A MIX OF FOUND OBJECTS, COMMUNITY CONTRIBUTIONS, AND MORE COVER HALF A BLOCK IN PENNSYLVANIA WITH BRIGHT HUES, TEXTURES, AND TILES OF ALL SORTS.

THE LABYRINTH OF THE GARDENS IS PACKED WITH SCULPTURES, HANDMADE ART, AND OTHER OBJECTS, AND IT'S NO WONDER THAT THE MAGIC GARDENS ARE NOT A PERMANENT ART INSTITUTION HOSTING LIVE ENTERTAINMENT AND PUBLIC WORKSHOPS RUN BY THE MAN HIMSELF, ZAGAR!

ADDRESS: 1020 SOUTH ST, PHILADELPHIA, PA 19147, UNITED STATES

PASSPORT STAMPS:

NOTES :

Cave of Kelpius

DESCRIPTION / THINGS TO DO :

THE CAVE OF KELPIUS SITS IN FAIRMOUNT PARK OF PHILADELPHIA, PENNSYLVANIA, ONE OF THE UNUSUAL PLACES TO SEE IN ONE OF THE MOST BEAUTIFUL STATES IN THE US.

IT IS AN ENHANCED CAVE OF SORTS, FITTED INTO A HILLSIDE, ITS ONE ENTRANCE MARKED BY A STONE FRAME. IT IS HERE THAT IT IS THOUGHT THAT THE FIRST MYSTIC CULT IN AMERICA LIVED IN THE 17TH CENTURY.

SUPPOSEDLY, THE CAVE WAS SETTLED BY JOHANNES KELPIUS, A SCHOLAR AND MYSTIC, WITH HIS 40 ALL-MALE FOLLOWERS IN 1694. HE BELIEVED THAT THE WORLD WOULD COME TO AN END THAT YEAR DUE TO HIS INTERPRETATION OF THE BOOK OF REVELATION.

THEY WERE ALSO CALLED, SIMPLY, THE HERMITS OF THE WISSAHICKON, WHICH LENDS ITSELF TO THE NAME OF THE AREA: HERMIT'S GLEN, MARKED IN PRESENT-DAY PENNSYLVANIA BY THE ROAD HERMIT LANE.

IN THE CAVE OF KELPIUS, THE GROUP PRACTICED ASTRONOMY AND USED THE SPACE TO MEET AND AS AN OBSERVATORY. THEY REMAINED THERE EVEN AFTER THE WORLD DID NOT END, AND THEY CONTINUED TO STUDY THE SKIES, MAKE MUSIC AND ART, AND EVEN HELP THE COMMUNITY.

IN 1708, KELPIUS DIED, AND THE GROUP LARGELY DISBANDED, WITH MANY REMAINING IN THE AREA TO SERVE AS LAWYERS AND DOCTORS. THE CAVE IS LARGELY DEMOLISHED NOW, WITH ONLY THE STONE STRUCTURE OUTSIDE REMAINING, BUT IT'S A FASCINATING VISIT STEEPED IN HISTORY.

ADDRESS: 777-795 HERMIT LN, PHILADELPHIA, PA 19128, UNITED STATES

PASSPORT STAMPS:

NOTES :

Carnegie Museum of Natural History

VISTED DATE :   SPRING ◯   SUMMER ◯   FALL ◯   WINTER ◯

WEATHER :   ☀️◯   ⛅◯   🌧️◯   🌨️◯   ⛈️◯   🌬️◯   🌡️TEMP :

FEE(S) :   RATING : ☆ ☆ ☆ ☆ ☆   WILL I RETURN?   YES / NO

LODGING :   WHO I WENT WITH :

DESCRIPTION / THINGS TO DO :

THE CARNEGIE MUSEUM OF NATURAL HISTORY WAS FOUNDED IN 1896 BY THE TITULAR ANDREW CARNEGIE, AN INDUSTRIALIST AND LOCAL OF PITTSBURGH, PENNSYLVANIA.

IT WAS HERE THAT HOUSED THE SCIENTISTS THAT DISCOVERED THE FIRST FOSSILS OF THE DIPLODOCUS CARNEGII DINOSAUR.

IT'S A FUN SPOT AND ONE OF THE COOLEST PLACES TO VISIT IN PA WITH FAMILY.

THROUGHOUT THE CARNEGIE MUSEUM OF NATURAL HISTORY, YOU'LL SEE EXHIBITS OF MINERALS, FOSSILS, GEMS, ANIMALS, AND MORE.

THE MUSEUM'S PRIDE IS HOUSING THE PLANET'S BIGGEST JURASSIC DINOSAUR COLLECTION, INCLUDING THE FIRST TYRANNOSAURUS REX SPECIMEN AND THE ONLY JUVENILE APATOSAURUS FOSSILS.

WHILE DINOSAURS ARE THE MAIN DRAW, TOPICS SUCH AS ARCHEOLOGY, HERPETOLOGY, AND ZOOLOGY ARE ALSO COVERED.

ADDRESS: 4400 FORBES AVE, PITTSBURGH, PA 15213, UNITED STATES

PASSPORT STAMPS:

NOTES :

Shofuso Japanese House and Garden

VISTED DATE :   SPRING ◯   SUMMER ◯   FALL ◯   WINTER ◯

WEATHER :   ☀◯ ⛅◯ 🌧◯ ❄◯ ⛈◯ 💨◯   🌡TEMP :

FEE(S) :   RATING : ☆ ☆ ☆ ☆ ☆   WILL I RETURN?   YES / NO

LODGING :   WHO I WENT WITH :

DESCRIPTION / THINGS TO DO :

THE SHOFUSO JAPANESE HOUSE AND GARDEN SITS CLOSE TO THE BASE OF PENNSYLVANIA'S SCHUYLKILL RIVER. IT IS A HIDDEN GEM AMONG TOURIST ATTRACTIONS, BUT ONE OF THE COUNTRY'S BEST EXAMPLES OF GENUINE JAPANESE DESIGN FROM CENTURIES AGO.

THE NAME "SHOFUSO" ROUGHLY MEANS "PINE BREEZE VILLA" AND WAS MADE AS PART OF A HOUSE IN THE GARDEN EXHIBIT FOR THE MUSEUM OF MODERN ART. THE SHOFUSO JAPANESE HOUSE AND GARDEN WAS MADE BY JUNZŌ YOSHIMURA, AN ARCHITECT, WHO BUILT IT IN JAPAN IN 1953.

IT WAS SENT AND ASSEMBLED IN NEW YORK THE FOLLOWING YEAR, GIVEN TO AMERICA AS A GIFT FROM JAPAN. FOR A WHILE, THE MUSEUM OF MODERN ART HELD ONTO IT, AND THEN THE EXHIBITION CLOSED AND IT WAS MOVED TO PHILADELPHIA, PENNSYLVANIA, IN 1958. THE HOUSE OF THE SHOFUSO JAPANESE HOUSE AND GARDEN IS DESIGNED FOLLOWING SHOIN-ZUKURI ARCHITECTURE AND PROPORTIONS. IT IS MEANT TO RESEMBLE A TEMPLE GUEST HOUSE, BOASTING A KITCHEN, TEA ROOM, AND BATH AND TOPPED WITH A ROOF OF HINOKI BARK THAT HAD TO BE SPECIALLY REQUESTED FROM THE NATIONAL FORESTRY AGENCY OF JAPAN.

THE GARDENS, ON THE OTHER HAND, ARE HOST TO A TEA GARDEN, COURTYARD GARDEN, KOI POND, AND A LITTLE ISLAND. VANDALISM AND ABANDONMENT LEFT THE SHOFUSO JAPANESE HOUSE AND GARDEN IN DISREPAIR FOR YEARS.

FAMOUS JAPANESE PAINTER HIROSHI SENJU HELPED REFURBISH IT IN 2007, DONATING 20 MURALS TO THE GROUNDS. NOW, THE PLACE IS VERY MUCH PERKED UP, AND IT'S ONE OF THE GREATEST TOURIST ATTRACTIONS IN THE STATE.

ADDRESS: LANSDOWNE DR &, HORTICULTURAL DR, PHILADELPHIA, PA 19131, UNITED STATES

PASSPORT STAMPS:

NOTES :

Mercer Museum and Fonthill Castle

VISTED DATE :   SPRING ⃝ SUMMER ⃝ FALL ⃝ WINTER ⃝

WEATHER :   ☀⃝ 🌤⃝ 🌧⃝ 🌨⃝ ⛈⃝ 🌬⃝   🌡TEMP :

FEE(S) :   RATING : ☆ ☆ ☆ ☆ ☆   WILL I RETURN?   YES / NO

LODGING :   WHO I WENT WITH :

DESCRIPTION / THINGS TO DO :

THE MERCER MUSEUM AND FONTHILL CASTLE ARE NEAR TO EACH OTHER AND ARE CLOSELY RELATED, MAKING THEM THE BEST PLACES TO VISIT IN PENNSYLVANIA BACK-TO-BACK. FONTHILL CASTLE WAS THE HOME OF HENRY CHAPMAN MERCER, A FAMOUS COLLECTOR, TILE MAKER, AND ARCHAEOLOGIST.

HE PLANNED THE HOUSE COMPLETELY, FROM THE EXTERIOR TO EACH INTERIOR ROOM, WHICH HE SKETCHED AND IMAGINED HIMSELF.

FONTHILL CASTLE WAS FINISHED IN 1912 AND IS MADE COMPLETELY FROM POURED CONCRETE, SOMEHOW ORNATE AND SOMEHOW IMPOSSIBLE TO CATEGORIZE FROM AN ARCHITECTURAL STANDPOINT.

THE USE OF PURE CONCRETE WAS DUE TO MERCER'S FEAR OF FIRES, WHICH DEVELOPED AFTER HE LOST SOME MEDIEVAL ARMOR THAT HE WAS STORING WHILE BUILDING THE MUSEUM TO THE GREAT BOSTON FIRE. PEOPLE MADE FUN OF HIM — BUT HE DEMONSTRATED THE EFFECTIVENESS OF SUCH CONSTRUCTION BY BUILDING A HUGE BONFIRE ON AN UPPER TERRACE AND ALLOWING IT TO RAGE, HIGH ENOUGH FOR ALL RESIDENTS OF THE SURROUNDING DOYLESTOWN TO SEE. WATCHMAKERS' GEARS, TORTOISESHELL COMB MAKERS' SUPPLIES, WHALERS' BOATS, BUTCHERS' INSTRUMENTS, A FAKE VAMPIRE HUNTING KIT, AND MORE. THE MUSEUM IS ALSO MADE FROM PURE CONCRETE AND HOUSES 55 EXHIBIT ROOMS THAT EACH CONCENTRATE ON DIFFERENT TRADES FROM PRE-INDUSTRIAL TIMES, SUCH AS FARMING, METALS-MITHING, MILLING, WOODWORKING, AND SEWING TOOLS. THERE ARE ALSO STRANGE OBJECTS LIKE UNORTHODOX FIRE ENGINES, A WHALEBOAT, GALLOWS, AND STOVE PLATES.

THE MUSEUM WAS OPENED IN 1916 AND HAS SINCE INCLUDED THE ADDITION OF A CHILDREN'S ROOM ON THE HIGHEST FLOOR.

ADDRESS: 525 E COURT ST, DOYLESTOWN, PA 18901, UNITED STATES

PASSPORT STAMPS:

NOTES :

Dutch Wonderland

VISTED DATE :   SPRING ○   SUMMER ○   FALL ○   WINTER ○

WEATHER :   ☀○   ⛅○   🌧○   ❄○   ⛈○   🌬○   🌡TEMP :

FEE(S) :   RATING : ☆ ☆ ☆ ☆ ☆   WILL I RETURN?   YES / NO

LODGING :   WHO I WENT WITH :

DESCRIPTION / THINGS TO DO :

DUTCH WONDERLAND IS ONE OF THE MOST FUN PLACES TO GO IF YOU HAVE CHILDREN, NICKNAMED A KINGDOM FOR KIDS AND SITUATED IN LANCASTER, PENNSYLVANIA.

IT IS A 48-ACRE AMUSEMENT PARK AND HAS BEEN OPENED SINCE 1963, EARNING — OVER TIME — A REPUTATION AS ONE OF THE WORLD'S GREATEST CHILDREN'S THEME PARKS.

THERE ARE MORE THAN 30 RIDES IN PENNSYLVANIA'S DUTCH WONDERLAND, INCLUDING ROLLER COASTERS, SLIDES, CASTLES, A THEMED WATER PARK CALLED DUKE'S LAGOON, AND LIVE PERFORMANCES AND SHOWS THAT WILL DELIGHT AND AMUSE!

THERE ARE PLENTY OF ACTIVITIES TO KEEP KIDS OCCUPIED THIS WEEKEND, SO BRING YOUR LITTLE ONES ALONG.

ADDRESS: 2249 LINCOLN HWY E, LANCASTER, PA 17602, UNITED STATES

PASSPORT STAMPS:

NOTES :

The Sonorous Stones of Ringing Rocks Park

VISTED DATE : SPRING ◯ SUMMER ◯ FALL ◯ WINTER ◯

WEATHER : ☀️◯ ⛅◯ 🌧️◯ 🌨️◯ ⛈️◯ 🌬️◯   🌡️TEMP :

FEE(S) : RATING : ☆ ☆ ☆ ☆ ☆   WILL I RETURN? YES / NO

LODGING :   WHO I WENT WITH :

DESCRIPTION / THINGS TO DO :

IF YOU'RE LOOKING FOR MUSICAL THINGS TO DO IN PENNSYLVANIA, BRING YOUR OWN HAMMERS AND COME TO THE SONOROUS STONES OF RINGING ROCKS PARK.

IT WAS FIRST "DISCOVERED" IN 1890 WHEN J. J. OTT PERFORMED FOR THE BUCKWAMPUM HISTORICAL SOCIETY WITH A CONCERT WHERE HE USED A UNIQUE INSTRUMENT: STONES, STRUCK WITH A HAMMER TO MAKE CLEAR BELL TONES!

THE ROCKS HAD BEEN TAKEN FROM UPPER BLACK EDDY IN PENNSYLVANIA, OR WHAT IS KNOWN NOW AS RINGING ROCKS PARK.

THE FIELD OF ROCK SPANS 7 ACRES AND IS MORE THAN 10 FEET DEEP WITH THESE ROCKS.

TESTS BY SCIENTISTS IN 1965 REVEALED THAT ALL THE ROCKS HERE RING AT DIFFERENT TONES, EVEN IF THOSE TONES ARE ONES THAT HUMAN EARS CAN'T HEAR.

AS FOR WHY THEY RING, THAT'S A MYSTERY THAT'S STILL UNSOLVED.

EVEN STRANGER, THE ROCKS LOSE THEIR MUSICAL ABILITY ONCE REMOVED FROM THE REST!

ADDRESS: RINGING ROCKS RD, UPPER BLACK EDDY, PA 18972, UNITED STATES

PASSPORT STAMPS:

NOTES :

Penn's Cave

VISTED DATE :   SPRING ◯ SUMMER ◯ FALL ◯ WINTER ◯

WEATHER : ☀◯ ⛅◯ 🌧◯ 🌨◯ ⛈◯ 🌬◯   🌡TEMP :

FEE(S) :   RATING : ☆ ☆ ☆ ☆ ☆   WILL I RETURN? YES / NO

LODGING :   WHO I WENT WITH :

DESCRIPTION / THINGS TO DO :

PENN'S CAVE IS SITUATED IN PENNSYLVANIA'S GREGG TOWNSHIP AND IS A SUBTERRANEAN WATERWAY IN AN INLET OF LAKE NITANEE THAT STRETCHES A QUARTER OF A MILE.

IT IS FILLED WITH THINGS TO SEE AND IS A LARGE PROPERTY WITH A 55-FOOT ROOF AND SEVEN BUILDINGS.

THE LIMESTONE CAVERN IS ON THE NATIONAL REGISTER OF HISTORIC PLACES AND IS HIGHLIGHTED BY PENN'S CAVE HOUSE, WHICH IS AN OFFICE FOR TOURS AND A PRIVATE RESIDENCE.

BOATS ARE THE BEST WAY TO EXPLORE, AND THEY BRING YOU THROUGH THE LONG CAVE TO SEE ORNATE FORMATIONS OF LIMESTONE, THE WORKING FARM WITH CATTLE, A WILDLIFE PARK, A BAT COLONY, THE HISTORIC BUILDINGS, AND THE GEOLOGY AND NATURAL FLORA AND FAUNA.

PENN'S CAVE OPENED IN PENNSYLVANIA IN 1885 AS A SHOW CAVE AND FEATURES FORMATIONS WITH GRAND NAMES LIKE ANGEL'S WING, THE STATUE OF LIBERTY, AND GARDEN OF THE GODS.

ADDRESS: 222 PENNS CAVE RD, CENTRE HALL, PA 16828, UNITED STATES

PASSPORT STAMPS:

NOTES :

The Franklin Institute and The Foucault Pendulum

VISTED DATE : SPRING ◯ SUMMER ◯ FALL ◯ WINTER ◯

WEATHER : ☀️◯ 🌥️◯ 🌧️◯ 🌨️◯ ⛈️◯ 🌬️◯   🌡️TEMP :

FEE(S) :   RATING : ☆ ☆ ☆ ☆ ☆   WILL I RETURN? YES / NO

LODGING :   WHO I WENT WITH :

DESCRIPTION / THINGS TO DO :

THE FRANKLIN INSTITUTE IS A HIGHLY POPULAR SCIENCE MUSEUM THAT IS ONE OF THE CHIEF CENTERS FOR PENNSYLVANIA'S SCIENTIFIC EDUCATION AND RESEARCH. IT IS THE SITE OF A NATIONAL MEMORIAL FOR BENJAMIN FRANKLIN, A WIDE RANGE OF FUN PERMANENT EXHIBITS THAT DIG INTO MANY DIFFERENT REALMS OF SCIENTIFIC TOPICS, AND A NUMBER OF FASCINATING AND EXCITING TEMPORARY EXHIBITS.

BUT EVEN IF SCIENCE MUSEUMS AREN'T YOUR IDEAL CHOICE FOR WHAT TO DO IN PENNSYLVANIA, YOU SHOULD STOP BY THE FRANKLIN INSTITUTE TO VIEW THE FOUCAULT PENDULUM. IT IS A MASSIVE FOUR-STORY CREATION THAT HANGS IN THE INSTITUTE'S CEILING, WHERE IT HAS BEEN FOR 80 YEARS.

BELIEVE IT OR NOT, SUCH STRUCTURES WERE ONCE TRENDY TO HAVE IN SCIENCE MUSEUMS!

THE FIRST PENDULUM OF THIS KIND WAS MADE BY LÉON FOUCAULT IN 1851, WHO CONSTRUCTED A 67-FOOT HEAVY PENDULUM AND HUNG IT FROM A CEILING OVER A CIRCULAR PROTRACTOR. THE DEVICE WOULD APPEAR TO SWING IN A CIRCLE THROUGHOUT THE DAY, BUT IT WAS NOT, ITSELF, MOVING — IT WAS THE EARTH'S ROTATION BENEATH IT THAT MOVED. THIS WAS FOUCAULT'S ELEGANT METHOD OF PROVIDING THAT THE EARTH ROTATES ON ITS AXIS.

NOW, THE FOUCAULT PENDULUM OF THE FRANKLIN INSTITUTE IS A GREAT WAY TO VIEW THE EXPERIMENT FOR YOURSELF. IT TOOK 11 PEOPLE TO INSTALL AND HANGS FROM A WIRE OF 85 FEET!

THE ORB SWINGS APPROXIMATELY EVERY 20 MINUTES, TAKING 10 SECONDS TO SWING BACK AND FORTH, KNOCKING OVER PEGS AROUND A CIRCLE AS IT GOES.

ADDRESS: 222 N 20TH ST, PHILADELPHIA, PA 19103, UNITED STATES

PASSPORT STAMPS:

NOTES :

Longwood Gardens

VISTED DATE :   SPRING ◯ SUMMER ◯ FALL ◯ WINTER ◯

WEATHER : ☀◯ 🌤◯ 🌧◯ 🌨◯ ⛈◯ 🌬◯   🌡TEMP :

FEE(S) :   RATING : ☆ ☆ ☆ ☆ ☆   WILL I RETURN? YES / NO

LODGING :   WHO I WENT WITH :

DESCRIPTION / THINGS TO DO :

THE LONGWOOD GARDENS IS ONE OF THE VERY BEST INSTITUTIONS FOR HORTICULTURE IN PENNSYLVANIA AND, IN FACT, THE ENTIRE COUNTRY.

IT'S ONE OF THE VACATION SPOTS YOU'LL NEED TO SPEND THIS WEEKEND IN TO EVEN BARELY EXPLORE — IT'S THAT LARGE!

THE LONGWOOD GARDENS BEGAN THEIR LIFE IN 1700 AS A QUAKER FARM. A CENTURY LATER, IT BECAME AN ARBORETUM, AND THEN BECAME A (STILL PUBLICLY OPEN) PRIVATE RESIDENCE IN 1906, WITH ARTIFACTS AND STRUCTURES MADE OR BROUGHT IN INSPIRED BY THE WORLD FAIR.

ATTRACTIONS INCLUDE A GIANT PIPE ORGAN WITH 10,010 PIPES, THE KING OF THE CONSERVATORY ENCEPHALARTOS WOODII PLANT THAT IS EXTINCT IN NATURE, AND A WATERLILY DISPLAY THAT BOASTS NINE POOLS OF DIFFERENT WATER-BASED FLORA.

THERE ARE MORE THAN 11,000 SPECIES OF FLORA IN THE 20 OUTDOOR GARDENS OF THE LONGWOOD GARDENS, AND 5,500 SPECIES OR SO INSIDE THE CONSERVATORY.

GREENHOUSES AND OTHER COLLECTIONS BOAST THEMES LIKE THE ORANGERY, THE PALM HOUSE, THE ORCHID HOUSE, AND ACACIA PASSAGE, AND THERE ARE NUMEROUS EXOTIC PLANTS FROM SOUTH AFRICA AND AUSTRALIA, TOO. SEASONAL EVENTS AND DISPLAYS, SPECIAL PERFORMANCES, WORKSHOPS, LECTURES, COURSES, AND A TUITION-FREE HORTICULTURAL DEGREE ARE ALL AVAILABLE. IT'S TRULY ONE OF THE GREATEST PLACES TO VISIT IN PA FOR NATURE LOVERS.

ADDRESS: 1001 LONGWOOD RD, KENNETT SQUARE, PA 19348, UNITED STATES

PASSPORT STAMPS:

NOTES :

Wharton Esherick Museum

VISTED DATE :   SPRING ◯   SUMMER ◯   FALL ◯   WINTER ◯

WEATHER :   ☀◯   🌤◯   🌧◯   ❄◯   ⛈◯   🌬◯   🌡TEMP :

FEE(S) :   RATING : ☆ ☆ ☆ ☆ ☆   WILL I RETURN?   YES / NO

LODGING :   WHO I WENT WITH :

DESCRIPTION / THINGS TO DO :

THE WHARTON ESHERICK MUSEUM IS A CELEBRATION OF THE WORKS AND CAREER OF THE TITULAR WHARTON ESHERICK, WHO WAS A DESIGN ARTIST AND SCULPTOR WITH SIGNIFICANT INFLUENCE IN THE STUDIO FURNITURE MOVEMENT OF THE 20TH CENTURY.

THE MUSEUM COVERS 12 ACRES OF LAND AND IS SET WITHIN WHAT WAS ONCE THE HILLTOP STUDIO OF THE ARTIST HIMSELF.

THE MUSEUM HAS ALSO EARNED THE HONOR OF BECOMING ONE OF PENNSYLVANIA'S NATIONAL HISTORIC LANDMARKS FOR ARCHITECTURE.

ESHERICK WORKED WITH WOOD AND CREATED ALL SORTS OF ARCHITECTURAL AND FURNITURE DESIGNS THAT USED NATURAL, FLOWING STYLES IN A BEAUTIFUL AESTHETIC. HE BUILT THE HOUSE HERE IN THIS SECLUDED LOCATION OVER THE COURSE OF 40 YEARS, BEGINNING HIS WORK IN 1926 IN THE WOODS OF PENNSYLVANIA.

IN THAT TIME, HE WOULD ADD DETAILS AND FURNISHINGS BASED ON HIS CURRENT STYLE, RANGING FROM THE ROUGHER ROOTS OF ARTS AND CRAFTS TO THE SMOOTH MODERNIST DESIGNS THAT WOULD BECOME HIS HALLMARK. ON THE SITE, YOU CAN SEE HIS WORKSHOP AND GARAGE, HIS STUDIO, AND MANY OF HIS WORKS.

HE FOUND A LOT OF STUFF TO DO WITH HIS CRAFT AND HIS PROLIFICNESS SHOWS!

ADDRESS: 1520 HORSE SHOE TRAIL, MALVERN, PA 19355, UNITED STATES

PASSPORT STAMPS:

NOTES :

Philadelphia Zoo

VISTED DATE :   SPRING ◯   SUMMER ◯   FALL ◯   WINTER ◯

WEATHER :   ☀◯   ⛅◯   🌧◯   🌨◯   ⛈◯   🌬◯   🌡TEMP :

FEE(S) :   RATING : ☆ ☆ ☆ ☆ ☆   WILL I RETURN?   YES / NO

LODGING :   WHO I WENT WITH :

DESCRIPTION / THINGS TO DO :

THE PHILADELPHIA ZOO SHOULD BE ON YOUR LIST OF WHAT TO SEE IN PENNSYLVANIA BECAUSE IT'S AMERICA'S OLDEST ZOO!

IT IS HOME TO OVER 1,300 INDIVIDUAL ANIMALS, INCLUDING MANY THAT ARE ENDANGERED OR RARE, HOUSED ACROSS 42 ACRES IN FAIRMOUNT PARK, PHILADELPHIA, PENNSYLVANIA.

THE PHILADELPHIA ZOO'S SELECTION OF ANIMALS INCLUDES LIZARDS, LIONS, PRIMATES, TIGERS, CAMELS, HORSES, PONIES, LORIKEETS, AND MORE.

UNIQUE AND FUN ACTIVITIES, LIKE THE AMAZON RAINFOREST CAROUSEL, MAKE FOR AN EXCITING TIME.

THE ZOO 360 ATTRACTION IS INCREDIBLY POPULAR, AND IT FEATURES MESH ELEVATED WALKWAYS WHERE ANIMALS WALK ABOVE YOUR HEAD!

ADDRESS: 3400 W GIRARD AVE, PHILADELPHIA, PA 19104, UNITED STATES

PASSPORT STAMPS:

NOTES :

The Barnes Foundation

Visted date :   SPRING ◯   SUMMER ◯   FALL ◯   WINTER ◯

Weather :   ☀️◯ ⛅◯ 🌧️◯ 🌨️◯ ⛈️◯ 🌬️◯   🌡️Temp :

Fee(s) :   Rating : ☆ ☆ ☆ ☆ ☆   Will I return?   YES / NO

Lodging :   Who I went with :

Description / Things to do :

The Barnes Foundation is an impeccable art gallery founded in 1922 by the titular Albert Barnes.

A chemist whose fortune came from drug development, Barnes fell in love with art and spent much of his wealth collecting art pieces that are now on display here.

The gallery is designed in such a way that it feels more like a wealthy Pennsylvania home than a museum or art collection, and it's one of the best places to visit in Pennsylvania for art lovers.

The Barnes Foundation features works by greats like Van Gogh, Renoir, Degas, Matisse, Cezanne, Rubes, El Greco, Rubens, Picasso, and Manet, with works spanning Impressionist, Modernist, African art, and many other styles.

The eclectic collection is arranged in Barnes' personal "wall ensembles" method.

Address: 2025 Benjamin Franklin Pkwy, Philadelphia, PA 19130, United States

Passport stamps:

NOTES :

State Museum of Pennsylvania

VISTED DATE :   SPRING ◯ SUMMER ◯ FALL ◯ WINTER ◯

WEATHER : ☀◯ ☁◯ 🌧◯ 🌨◯ ⛈◯ 🌬◯   🌡TEMP :

FEE(S) :   RATING : ☆ ☆ ☆ ☆ ☆   WILL I RETURN? YES / NO

LODGING :   WHO I WENT WITH :

DESCRIPTION / THINGS TO DO :

THE STATE MUSEUM OF PENNSYLVANIA'S MAIN GOAL IS THE PRESERVATION OF THE HISTORY AND CULTURE OF THE STATE.

IT IS ALSO CALLED THE WILLIAM PENN MEMORIAL MUSEUM THANKS TO THE FACT THAT IT HOUSES A LARGE STATUE OF THE MAN IN ITS MAIN HALL.

LOCATED ON NORTH STREET OF HARRISBURG, IT'S ONE OF THE CHIEF POINTS OF INTEREST TO HEAD TO IF YOU WANT TO GAIN MORE INSIGHT INTO THE STATE.

THE STATE MUSEUM OF PENNSYLVANIA SPANS FOUR FLOORS AND HOUSES OVER THREE MILLION EXHIBITED ITEMS.

THESE OBJECTS AND ARTIFACTS COVER MANY DIFFERENT TOPICS, INCLUDING THE CIVIL WAR, FOSSILS, DIORAMAS AND ART, AND STATE HISTORY FROM PREHISTORIC TIMES TILL NOW.

THERE IS ALSO A PLANETARIUM THAT PUTS ON SHOWS LIKE SOLAR SUPERSTORMS, DYNAMIC EARTH, AND GROSSOLOGY AND YOU.

ADDRESS: 300 NORTH ST, HARRISBURG, PA 17120, UNITED STATES

PASSPORT STAMPS:

NOTES :

Indian Echo Caverns

VISTED DATE : SPRING ◯ SUMMER ◯ FALL ◯ WINTER ◯

WEATHER : ☀◯ 🌤◯ 🌧◯ 🌨◯ ⛈◯ 🌬◯ 🌡TEMP :

FEE(S) : RATING : ☆ ☆ ☆ ☆ ☆ WILL I RETURN? YES / NO

LODGING : WHO I WENT WITH :

DESCRIPTION / THINGS TO DO :

THE INDIAN ECHO CAVERNS ARE PRETTY MUCH THE DEFINITION OF THINGS TO DO IN PENNSYLVANIA, A TOURIST TRAP HOTSPOT THAT IS CROWDED AND PACKED WITH OVERSOLD COMMERCIALIZATION.

HOWEVER, IT'S ALSO A FUN VISIT EVEN DESPITE THIS, AND THE LIMESTONE CAVES ARE BEAUTIFUL ENOUGH TO WARRANT A TRIP WHILE YOU'RE IN PENNSYLVANIA.

THE STORY OF THE INDIAN ECHO CAVERNS IS PRETTY INTERESTING, AND IT HAS LIVED MANY LIVES.

IT BEGAN AS A SHELTER AND STORAGE SITE FOR SUSQUEHANNOCK INDIANS, A SPOT FOR FRENCH FUR TRAPPERS TO HIDE OUT, AND EVENTUALLY A BEAUTIFUL LOCATION FOR COMMODIFICATION AS A TOURIST DRAW.

THOUGH IT'S A LITTLE TRANSPARENT IN ITS INTENTIONS, THE CAVERNS ARE AMONG THE STATE'S MOST SCENIC PLACES AND THERE'S A REASON THEY'VE SURVIVED WORLD WAR II AND THE GREAT DEPRESSION TO LIVE ON IN POPULARITY TODAY!

ADDRESS: 368 MIDDLETOWN RD, HUMMELSTOWN, PA 17036, UNITED STATES

PASSPORT STAMPS:

NOTES :

The Hershey Story

VISTED DATE :   SPRING ◯ SUMMER ◯ FALL ◯ WINTER ◯

WEATHER :   ☀◯ ⛅◯ 🌧◯ 🌨◯ ⛈◯ 🌬◯   🌡TEMP :

FEE(S) :   RATING : ☆ ☆ ☆ ☆ ☆   WILL I RETURN?   YES / NO

LODGING :   WHO I WENT WITH :

DESCRIPTION / THINGS TO DO :

THE HERSHEY STORY, AS ITS NAME SUGGESTS, IS A FUN MUSEUM DEDICATED TO TELLING THE STORY OF HERSHEY'S CHOCOLATES AND ITS FOUNDER, MILTON HERSHEY.

IT'S ONE OF THE MANY PENNSYLVANIA ATTRACTIONS DEDICATED TO THE COMPANY AND IS AN INSPIRING, FAMILY-FRIENDLY GLIMPSE INTO THE RISE, STRUGGLES, AND SUCCESSES OF HERSHEY HIMSELF.

AT THE HERSHEY STORY, YOU'LL SEE ALL SORTS OF EXHIBITS, INCLUDING MANY INTERACTIVE DISPLAYS, THAT FEATURE TALES OF HERSHEY, THE STORY OF CHOCOLATE AND ITS HISTORY, AND EVEN A CHOCOLATE LAB WHERE YOU CAN MAKE YOUR OWN CHOCOLATE.

DON'T FORGET TO TRY SOME OF THE AVAILABLE CHOCOLATE TASTE TESTS, FEATURING SWEET TREATS FROM PENNSYLVANIA, AMERICA, AND THE WORLD!

ADDRESS: 63 W CHOCOLATE AVE, HERSHEY, PA 17033, UNITED STATES

PASSPORT STAMPS:

NOTES :

Susquehanna Art Museum

VISTED DATE :   SPRING ◯   SUMMER ◯   FALL ◯   WINTER ◯

WEATHER :   ☀◯ ⛅◯ 🌧◯ 🌨◯ ⛈◯ 🌬◯   🌡 TEMP :

FEE(S) :   RATING : ☆ ☆ ☆ ☆ ☆   WILL I RETURN?   YES / NO

LODGING :   WHO I WENT WITH :

DESCRIPTION / THINGS TO DO :

THE SUSQUEHANNA ART MUSEUM IS THE ONLY DEDICATED ART MUSEUM IN CENTRAL PENNSYLVANIA.

IT OPENED IN 1989 AND WAS FOUNDED BY ART EDUCATORS, SHOWCASING WORKS BY LOCAL AND INTERNATIONAL ARTISTS ALIKE.

THERE ARE MANY THINGS TO SEE IN THE SUSQUEHANNA ART MUSEUM, WITH EXHIBITS LIKE TOWARDS A NEW/OLD ARCHITECTURE, FOUND IN TRANSLATION, THE EDGELESS DIVIDE, QUILTS 20/20, AND WORKS BY BEARDEN AND PICASSO.

THE MUSEUM MOVED TO A NEW LOCATION IN 2015 AND HAS BEEN THRIVING EVER SINCE — A PERFECT STOP ON YOUR SITE SEEING ADVENTURES!

ADDRESS: 1401 N 3RD ST, HARRISBURG, PA 17102, UNITED STATES

PASSPORT STAMPS:

NOTES :

Railroad Museum of Pennsylvania

VISTED DATE :   SPRING ◯ SUMMER ◯ FALL ◯ WINTER ◯

WEATHER :   ☀️◯ 🌤️◯ 🌧️◯ 🌨️◯ ⛈️◯ 💨◯   🌡️ TEMP :

FEE(S) :   RATING : ☆ ☆ ☆ ☆ ☆   WILL I RETURN?   YES / NO

LODGING :   WHO I WENT WITH :

DESCRIPTION / THINGS TO DO :

THE RAILROAD MUSEUM OF PENNSYLVANIA IS ONE OF THE COOLEST PLACES TO SEE FOR LOCOMOTIVE ENTHUSIASTS.

SPANNING 18 ACRES, IT CAN BE FOUND IN THE AMISH COUNTRYSIDE AND IS HOME TO OVER 100 DIFFERENT RAILROAD CARS AND LOCOMOTIVES.

IT CONTAINS MORE THAN 17,000 ARTIFACTS RELATED TO LOCOMOTIVES, INCLUDING SIGNAL EQUIPMENT, UNIFORMS, ARTWORK, TICKETS, TOOLS, SIGNS, AND MORE.

THE RAILROAD MUSEUM OF PENNSYLVANIA OPENED IN 1975 AND SERVES AS AN EDUCATIONAL AND INFORMATION LOCATION, TEACHING OTHERS ABOUT THE HISTORY OF RAILROADS IN THE STATE.

IT BOASTS INTERACTIVE EXHIBITS SUCH AS THE EXPLORATION OF A RAILCAR, LOCOMOTIVE SIMULATIONS, AND RESTORATION SHOP VIEWING.

THERE IS ALSO A LARGE ARCHIVAL LIBRARY FOR PERUSAL.

ADDRESS: 300 GAP RD, STRASBURG, PA 17579, UNITED STATES

PASSPORT STAMPS:

NOTES :

Brandywine Conservancy and Museum of Art

VISTED DATE :   SPRING ◯   SUMMER ◯   FALL ◯   WINTER ◯

WEATHER :   ☀️◯   🌤️◯   🌧️◯   ❄️◯   ⛈️◯   🌬️◯   🌡️TEMP :

FEE(S) :   RATING : ☆ ☆ ☆ ☆ ☆   WILL I RETURN?   YES / NO

LODGING :   WHO I WENT WITH :

DESCRIPTION / THINGS TO DO :

THE BRANDYWINE CONSERVANCY AND MUSEUM OF ART WAS CREATED TO PROTECT THE HISTORIC VALUE OF BRANDYWINE VALLEY, PENNSYLVANIA FROM INDUSTRIAL DEVELOPMENT THAT WOULD ALTER THE LANDSCAPE AND DEVASTATE THE CHARACTER AND WATER SUPPLIES OF THE AREA.

IN 1967, LOCAL RESIDENTS PURCHASED THE LAND AND TURNED IT INTO BRANDYWINE CONSERVANCY.

SINCE ITS EARLY DAYS, IT HAS GROWN TO PROTECT OVER 64,500 ACRES OF THE STATE AND BEYOND FROM DEVELOPMENT, CONTINUING TO PREACH AND ADVOCATE FOR RESPONSIBLE AND SUSTAINABLE LAND USE.

THE BRANDYWINE RIVER MUSEUM OF ART WAS OPENED IN 1971 THEN OPENED AND GREW INTO ONE OF THE STATE'S MOST REPUTABLE TOURIST ATTRACTIONS.

IT SEEKS GENUINE AMERICAN ART FROM THE LOCAL REGION AND HOUSES AN INCREDIBLE AND HIGH-QUALITY COLLECTION OF SUCH WORKS, INCLUDING ONES BY PYLE, THE WYETHS, DURAND, WEST, HARNETT, CHALFANT, STUART, RICHARDS, HARBERLE, PIPPIN, AND MORE.

GOING SIGHTSEEING ALONG THE CONSERVANCY'S LAND AND THEN POPPING IN TO VISIT THE MUSEUM IS A FANTASTIC WAY TO SEE MANY GREAT VACATION SPOTS AT ONCE.

ADDRESS: 1 HOFFMANS MILL RD, CHADDS FORD, PA 19317, UNITED STATES

PASSPORT STAMPS:

NOTES :

Lake Tobias Wildlife Park

VISTED DATE :   SPRING ○ SUMMER ○ FALL ○ WINTER ○

WEATHER :   ☀○ ☁○ 🌧○ 🌨○ ⛈○ 🌬○   🌡TEMP :

FEE(S) :   RATING : ☆ ☆ ☆ ☆ ☆   WILL I RETURN?   YES / NO

LODGING :   WHO I WENT WITH :

DESCRIPTION / THINGS TO DO :

LAKE TOBIAS WILDLIFE PARK WAS ESTABLISHED IN 1965 BY J. R. TOBIAS, WHO CREATED THE PARK AS A RETIREMENT HOBBY.

FROM THAT HUMBLE ORIGIN, IT HAS GROWN INTO ONE OF THE FAMOUS LANDMARKS OF THINGS TO DO IN PA!

THOUGH TOBIAS' PASSIONS LAY IN ANIMALS AND AGRICULTURE, HE WOUND UP OPTING FOR MORE PRACTICAL CAREER PATHS INSTEAD.

SERENDIPITOUSLY, THE SKILLS HE GAINED IN HIS CAREER ALLOWED HIM TO PUT HIS KNOWLEDGE TO USE AND CONSTRUCT THE PARK HIMSELF!

TODAY, SIX OF TOBIAS' CHILDREN AND ONE OF HIS GRANDCHILDREN RUN THE LAKE TOBIAS WILDLIFE PARK IN PENNSYLVANIA, WHICH ATTRACTS AN IMPRESSIVE 180,000 ANNUAL GUESTS.

THERE ARE LOTS OF ACTIVITIES YOU AND YOUR FAMILY CAN TAKE PART IN HERE, INCLUDING RIDES IN OPEN-AIR SAFARI VEHICLES, NUMEROUS THEMED FACILITIES AND EXHIBITS FOR DIFFERENT ANIMALS, A 500-GALLON AQUARIUM, AND MORE.

ADDRESS: 760 TOBIAS RD, HALIFAX, PA 17032, UNITED STATES

PASSPORT STAMPS:

NOTES :

Chanticleer

VISTED DATE :　　　　　　SPRING ◯　SUMMER ◯　FALL ◯　WINTER ◯

WEATHER :　☀️◯　⛅◯　🌧️◯　🌨️◯　⛈️◯　🌬️◯　🌡️TEMP :

FEE(S) :　　　　RATING : ☆ ☆ ☆ ☆ ☆　　WILL I RETURN?　YES / NO

LODGING :　　　　　　　WHO I WENT WITH :

DESCRIPTION / THINGS TO DO :

AS THE GARDEN CAPITAL OF PENNSYLVANIA AND AMERICA, PHILADELPHIA HAS ITS FAIR SHARE OF PLACES OF INTEREST RELATED TO GARDENS AND GARDENING.

CHANTICLEER, A PLEASURE GARDEN, IS ONE OF THEM.

IT DATES BACK TO THE EARLY YEARS OF THE 20TH CENTURY WHEN THE LAND WAS PURCHASED BY THE ROSENGARTEN FAMILY AS THEIR ESTATE.

THE BOTANICAL GARDENS, SPANNING 48 ACRES, WOULD BECOME PROMINENT IN PENNSYLVANIA AS A PUBLIC ATTRACTION AND ONE OF THE STATE'S BEAUTIFUL PLACES.

"CHANTICLEER" IS FRENCH FOR "ROOSTER", AND YOU'LL SEE LOTS OF ROOSTER MOTIFS AND DESIGNED AROUND CHANTICLEER.

WITH LARGE LAWNS, A POND, MULTIPLE GARDENS, AND FORESTED AREAS, YOU'LL BE ABLE TO SPOT FLORA SUCH AS BLACK-EYED SUSANS, ORNAMENTAL GRASS, AND DAISIES, AS WELL AS FAUNA LIKE GOLDFINCHES, GREEN HERONS, WRENS, AND HUMMINGBIRDS.

PLANTS FROM ALL OVER THE WORLD ARE ARRANGED THROUGHOUT CHANTICLEER, ALLOWING YOU TO IMMERSE YOURSELF IN A MIX OF LOCAL AND EXOTIC FLORA.

ADDRESS: 786 CHURCH RD, WAYNE, PA 19087, UNITED STATES

PASSPORT STAMPS:

NOTES :

Lackawanna Coal Mine

VISTED DATE :   SPRING ◯ SUMMER ◯ FALL ◯ WINTER ◯

WEATHER : ☀◯ ⛅◯ 🌧◯ 🌨◯ ⛈◯ 🌬◯   🌡TEMP :

FEE(S) :   RATING : ☆ ☆ ☆ ☆ ☆   WILL I RETURN? YES / NO

LODGING :   WHO I WENT WITH :

DESCRIPTION / THINGS TO DO :

THE LACKAWANNA COAL MINE WAS ONCE A WORKING COAL MINE, AND IT HAS A DARK HISTORY THAT SETS A MOODY TONE OVER THIS PORTION OF SCRANTON, PENNSYLVANIA.

MINERS HERE FACED AWFUL CONDITIONS IN PASSAGEWAYS AND TUNNELS, WITH CHILDREN AND ADULTS ALL WORKING HERE IN DEPLORABLE, DANGEROUS, AND POTENTIALLY DEADLY STATES.

TOURS OF THE LACKAWANNA COAL MINE BRING YOU DOWN INTO THE CLARK COAL VEIN.

YOU'LL LEARN ABOUT ANTHRACITE MINING, THEN MOVE ONTO OTHER VEINS THAT CAN TEACH YOU ABOUT FAULT ROOMS, THE FIRE BOSS, SMALL VEIN WORK, VENTILATION AND AIR DOORS, EXITS, NIPPERS, AND MORE.

THE MINE ITSELF CLOSED IN 1966 AND WAS REOPENED AS A MUSEUM IN 1978, WHERE IT IS NOW ONE OF PENNSYLVANIA'S PLACES TO GO.

ADDRESS: BALD MOUNTAIN RD, SCRANTON, PA 18504, UNITED STATES

PASSPORT STAMPS:

NOTES :

Edgar Allan Poe National Historic Site

VISITED DATE :   SPRING ◯   SUMMER ◯   FALL ◯   WINTER ◯

WEATHER :   ☀️◯ 🌥◯ 🌧◯ 🌨◯ ⛈◯ 🌬◯   🌡TEMP :

FEE(S) :   RATING : ☆ ☆ ☆ ☆ ☆   WILL I RETURN?   YES / NO

LODGING :   WHO I WENT WITH :

DESCRIPTION / THINGS TO DO :

THE EDGAR ALLAN POE NATIONAL HISTORIC SITE IS RATHER FASCINATING AS A SPOT IN PENNSYLVANIA, MOSTLY BECAUSE THE TITULAR POET ONLY LIVED IN THE STATE FOR A YEAR.

IN 1843, HE AND HIS WIFE MOVED INTO A HOME IN PHILADELPHIA, WHERE HE WROTE "THE GOLD BUG" AND "THE TELL-TALE HEART".

ALMOST A CENTURY LATER, A DIE-HARD FAN OF POE'S PURCHASED THE HOME AND DECIDED TO TURN IT INTO A MUSEUM.

WHEN THAT FAN PASSED AWAY, THE CITY OF PHILADELPHIA RECEIVED IT, AND IT BECAME A NATIONAL HISTORIC SITE.

THERE ARE THREE PERMANENT EXHIBITS AND TWO ROTATING EXHIBITS AT THE EDGAR ALLAN POE NATIONAL HISTORIC SITE, EACH LETTING YOU LOOK IN-DEPTH INTO HIS LIFE, TIMES, AND CAREER.

FOR LITERATURE LOVERS, A TRIP HERE IS ONE OF THE MOST FUN THINGS TO DO IN PENNSYLVANIA!

ADDRESS: 532 N 7TH ST, PHILADELPHIA, PA 19123, UNITED STATES

PASSPORT STAMPS:

NOTES :

National Civil War Museum

VISTED DATE :   SPRING ◯ SUMMER ◯ FALL ◯ WINTER ◯

WEATHER : ☀️◯ ⛅◯ 🌧️◯ 🌨️◯ ⛈️◯ 🌬️◯   🌡️TEMP :

FEE(S) :   RATING : ☆ ☆ ☆ ☆ ☆   WILL I RETURN?   YES / NO

LODGING :   WHO I WENT WITH :

DESCRIPTION / THINGS TO DO :

FOR HISTORY NERDS, A TRIP TO THE NATIONAL CIVIL WAR MUSEUM IN PENNSYLVANIA IS A MUST-DO.

IT IS DEDICATED TO TELLING THE TALE OF THE AMERICAN CIVIL WAR WITH THE USE OF 24,000 ITEMS AND ARTIFACTS HOUSED ACROSS TWO FLOORS AND 17 GALLERIES.

THE NATIONAL CIVIL WAR MUSEUM TELLS THE STORY OF THE WAR IN AS OBJECTIVE A MANNER AS POSSIBLE, AND AS A SMITHSONIAN AFFILIATE, YOU KNOW IT DOES THE JOB WELL.

THE GALLERIES BEGIN THE TALE OF THE CIVIL WAR IN 1850, PROJECTING THE TENSIONS THAT LED UP TO THE WAR IN 1861, AND ALL THE WAY UP TO 1876, TO SHOWCASE THE AFTERMATH THAT FOLLOWED THE WAR'S END IN 1865.

ADDRESS: 1 LINCOLN CIR, HARRISBURG, PA 17103, UNITED STATES

PASSPORT STAMPS:

NOTES :

Wagner Free Institute of Science

VISTED DATE : SPRING ◯ SUMMER ◯ FALL ◯ WINTER ◯

WEATHER : ☀️◯ ⛅◯ 🌧️◯ 🌨️◯ ⛈️◯ 🌬️◯ 🌡️TEMP :

FEE(S) : RATING : ☆ ☆ ☆ ☆ ☆ WILL I RETURN? YES / NO

LODGING : WHO I WENT WITH :

DESCRIPTION / THINGS TO DO :

THE WAGNER FREE INSTITUTE OF SCIENCE IS ONE OF THE MAIN PENNSYLVANIA ATTRACTIONS FOR GENUINE SCIENTIFIC LEARNING AND STUDY, OFFERING LECTURES AND CLASSES THAT ARE AMONG THE FREE THINGS TO DO IN PENNSYLVANIA.

THE TRADITION OF SUCH LESSONS BEGAN WITH WILLIAM WAGNER HIMSELF, WHO CONDUCTED FREE INFORMAL SCIENCE LESSONS OUT OF HIS HOME.

WAGNER'S CLASSES GREW SO POPULAR THAT HE OPENED THE WAGNER FREE INSTITUTE OF SCIENCE IN ORDER TO EXPAND.

WITHIN, NATURAL HISTORY COLLECTIONS BELONGING TO THE MAN WERE DISPLAYED, AND WAGER'S LESSONS CONTINUED.

WHEN HE PASSED AWAY, HIS LEGACY WAS CARRIED ON BY JOSEPH LEIDY, A BIOLOGIST, WHO EXPANDED ON THE RESEARCH AVAILABLE AND PERPETUATED WAGNER'S BELIEF THAT EDUCATION SHOULD BE ACCESSIBLE TO ALL.

ADDRESS: 1700 W MONTGOMERY AVE, PHILADELPHIA, PA 19121, UNITED STATES

PASSPORT STAMPS:

NOTES :

Flight 93 National Memorial

VISTED DATE :   SPRING ◯ SUMMER ◯ FALL ◯ WINTER ◯

WEATHER :   ☀️◯ 🌥️◯ 🌧️◯ 🌨️◯ ⛈️◯ 🌬️◯   🌡️TEMP :

FEE(S) :   RATING : ☆ ☆ ☆ ☆ ☆   WILL I RETURN?   YES / NO

LODGING :   WHO I WENT WITH :

DESCRIPTION / THINGS TO DO :

THE FLIGHT 93 NATIONAL MEMORIAL WAS CREATED TO PAY RESPECTS TO THE BRAVE PASSENGERS
AND CREW OF UNITED FLIGHT 93, ONE OF THE HIJACKED PLANES ON SEPTEMBER 11, 2001.

FOUR TERRORISTS OF AL-QAEDA GOT ONBOARD WITH THE GOAL OF CRASHING THE PLANE INTO THE
CAPITOL BUILDING, BUT THE CREW THWARTED THEM AND DIVERTED THE PLANE INTO A HILL IN PEN-
NSYLVANIA.

THERE WERE NO SURVIVORS ON THE PLANE, BUT GREATER TRAGEDY WAS AVERTED THANKS TO THEIR
SELFLESS COURAGE.

THE FLIGHT 93 NATIONAL MEMORIAL IS ONE OF THE KEY THINGS TO SEE TO GET THE WHOLE STORY OF
THE DAY, WITH INTERACTIVE INFORMATION, A WALKING PATH, A MEMORIAL WALL, AND EVEN PHONE
CALLS MADE BY PASSENGERS TO THEIR LOVED ONES BACK HOME AS THE PLANE WENT DOWN.

IT'S A SOBERING EXPERIENCE AND IS ALSO ONE OF THE STATE'S FREE THINGS TO DO, CHARGING NO
ADMISSION FEE.

ADDRESS: 6424 LINCOLN HWY, STOYSTOWN, PA 15563, UNITED STATES

PASSPORT STAMPS:

NOTES :

King of Prussia Mall

VISTED DATE :　　　　　　SPRING ◯　SUMMER ◯　FALL ◯　WINTER ◯

WEATHER :　☀ ◯　🌥 ◯　🌧 ◯　🌨 ◯　⛈ ◯　🌬 ◯　🌡 TEMP :

FEE(S) :　　　RATING : ☆ ☆ ☆ ☆ ☆　　WILL I RETURN?　YES / NO

LODGING :　　　　　　　WHO I WENT WITH :

DESCRIPTION / THINGS TO DO :

IF YOU'RE LOOKING FOR WHAT TO DO IN THE STATE OF PENNSYLVANIA TO SHOP TILL YOU DROP, THE KING OF PRUSSIA MALL – WHICH IS AMERICA'S SECOND-LARGEST – IS A GREAT STOP THIS WEEKEND.

MORE THAN 400 RESTAURANTS, BOUTIQUES, AND SHOPS FILL THE INTERIOR, WHICH MEASURES MORE THAN 2.6 MILLION SQUARE FEET IN SIZE.

THE ICONIC KING OF PRUSSIA MALL FEATURES A MIX OF LOCAL SHOPS AND COMMON LARGE RETAILERS, SUCH AS NORDSTROM, NEIMAN MARCUS, DICK'S SPORTING GOODS, BLOOMINGDALES, LORD AND TAYLOR, AND MACY'S.

THERE IS ALSO AN IFLY SKYDIVING CENTER AND A UNITED ARTISTS THEATRES BRANCH FOR FURTHER ENJOYMENT.

ADDRESS: 160 N GULPH RD, KING OF PRUSSIA, PA 19406, UNITED STATES

PASSPORT STAMPS:

NOTES :

Eisenhower National Historic Site

VISTED DATE :   SPRING ◯   SUMMER ◯   FALL ◯   WINTER ◯

WEATHER :   ☀◯   ☁◯   🌧◯   🌨◯   ⛈◯   🌬◯   🌡TEMP :

FEE(S) :   RATING : ☆ ☆ ☆ ☆ ☆   WILL I RETURN?   YES / NO

LODGING :   WHO I WENT WITH :

DESCRIPTION / THINGS TO DO :

THE EISENHOWER NATIONAL HISTORIC SITE WAS THE LOCATION OF THE FARM AND HOUSE OF 34TH UNITED STATES PRESIDENT DWIGHT D. EISENHOWER, NEXT TO THE GETTYSBURG BATTLEFIELD, WRAPPING TWO PENNSYLVANIA TOURIST ATTRACTIONS IN ONE PLACE.

THE HOUSE ITSELF WAS A WEEKEND AND VACATION HOME FOR THE PRESIDENT AND HIS WIFE, AND THEY RETIRED HERE IN 1961.

IN 1967, THEY DONATED THE PROPERTY TO THE GOVERNMENT.

THE PEACEFUL ATMOSPHERE OF THE EISENHOWER NATIONAL HISTORIC SITE EVOKES THE SAME CALM THAT THE PRESIDENT AND HIS WIFE ENJOYED ON THEIR BREAKS.

TOURS AND TALKS TEACH YOU ABOUT THE PLACE, BRINGING YOU THROUGH THE HOUSE, FARM, GARDENS, PUTTING GREEN, BARNS, SKEET RANGE, AND TEAHOUSE WHILE TELLING YOU ABOUT SECRET SERVICE OPERATIONS AND WORLD WAR II.

ADDRESS: 243 EISENHOWER FARM RD, GETTYSBURG, PA 17325, UNITED STATES

PASSPORT STAMPS:

NOTES :

Steamtown National Historic Site

VISTED DATE :   SPRING ◯ SUMMER ◯ FALL ◯ WINTER ◯

WEATHER :   ☀️◯ 🌤️◯ 🌧️◯ 🌨️◯ ⛈️◯ 🌬️◯   🌡️ TEMP :

FEE(S) :   RATING : ☆ ☆ ☆ ☆ ☆   WILL I RETURN? YES / NO

LODGING :   WHO I WENT WITH :

DESCRIPTION / THINGS TO DO :

THE STEAMTOWN NATIONAL HISTORIC SITE IS A MUSEUM DEDICATED TO THE HISTORY OF STEAM RAILROAD INNOVATION, TRANSPORTATION, AND THE PEOPLE BEHIND IT.

IT IS SITUATED IN AN OLD TRAIN YARD IN THE DOWNTOWN AREA OF SCRANTON, PENNSYLVANIA, AND HOUSES THE COLLECTION OF NEW JERSEY SEAFOOD MAGNATE F. NELSON BLOUNT.

THE STEAMTOWN NATIONAL HISTORIC SITE FEELS ALIVE AND WELL WITH THE FIREBOX, HOT STEAM, AND BELLS AND WHISTLES AS ONE-TON DRIVE RODS PUSH TRAIN WHEELS AND VIBRATE THE GROUND, CHUFFING OUT OF SMOKESTACKS.

YOU CAN RELIVE THE FANTASTIC 1920S ERA OF STEAM TRAINS AND VISIT INTERACTIVE DISPLAYS, A WORKING ROUNDHOUSE, A REPAIR SHOP, AND EVEN ARCHIVES.

THIS IS ONE OF THE ONLY PLACES TO VISIT IN PENNSYLVANIA FOR LOCOMOTIVE ENTHUSIASTS!

ADDRESS: 350 CLIFF ST, SCRANTON, PA 18503, UNITED STATES

PASSPORT STAMPS:

NOTES :

Presque Isle State Park

VISTED DATE :   SPRING ○ SUMMER ○ FALL ○ WINTER ○

WEATHER :   ☀️○ 🌥️○ 🌧️○ 🌨️○ ⛈️○ 🌬️○   🌡️TEMP :

FEE(S) :   RATING : ☆ ☆ ☆ ☆ ☆   WILL I RETURN?   YES / NO

LODGING :   WHO I WENT WITH :

DESCRIPTION / THINGS TO DO :

IF YOU'RE LOOKING FOR MORE RELAXING AND FREE THINGS TO DO IN THE STATE OF PENNSYLVANIA, ONE OF THE RELEVANT POINTS OF INTEREST IS PRESQUE ISLE STATE PARK.

SITUATED ON A PENINSULA ON PRESQUE ISLE BAY, IT BOASTS MANY DIFFERENT HIKING TRAILS AND A WHOPPING 11 MILES OF BEACH SPACE ON 3,200 ACRES OF LAND.

THERE ARE PLENTY OF ACTIVITIES TO TAKE PART IN AT PRESQUE ISLE STATE PARK.

YOU CAN SUNBATHE, SWIM, FLY KITES, COLLECT SEA GLASS, OR ATTEND LIVE PERFORMANCES, CONCERTS, AND EVENTS.

THERE IS ALSO THE TOM RIDGE ENVIRONMENTAL CENTER AT THE PARK'S ENTRANCE, WHICH PROVIDES INFORMATION ON LOCAL ECOSYSTEMS AND HISTORY AND PROVIDES A 75-FOOT OBSERVATION DECK TO USE FOR GREAT VIEWS.

ADDRESS: 301 PENINSULA DR, ERIE, PA 16505, UNITED STATES

PASSPORT STAMPS:

NOTES :

Allegheny Portage Railroad

VISTED DATE :   SPRING ◯ SUMMER ◯ FALL ◯ WINTER ◯

WEATHER :   ☀️◯ ⛅◯ 🌧️◯ 🌨️◯ ⛈️◯ 💨◯   🌡️TEMP :

FEE(S) :   RATING : ☆ ☆ ☆ ☆ ☆   WILL I RETURN? YES / NO

LODGING :   WHO I WENT WITH :

DESCRIPTION / THINGS TO DO :

THE ALLEGHENY PORTAGE RAILROAD WAS THE VERY FIRST RAILROAD TO BE BUILT THROUGH THE ALLEGHENY MOUNTAINS IN CENTRAL PENNSYLVANIA.

THIS MODERN INCLINED PLANE RAILROAD WAS CONSIDERED A TECHNOLOGICAL WONDER IN ITS DAY AND OPERATED BETWEEN 1834-1854, PLAYING A CRITICAL ROLE IN OPENING THE INTERIOR OF THE CO-UNTRY TO THE NEW SETTLEMENT.

LOCATED IN SOUTHWESTERN PENNSYLVANIA, APPROXIMATELY 12 MILES WEST OF ALTOONA, THE RAILROAD PROVIDES TRAIN ENTHUSIASTS AND HISTORY BUFFS AN OPPORTUNITY TO LEARN ABOUT OUR NATION'S RAILROAD HISTORY.

THE PARK FEATURES SEVERAL ATTRACTIONS, INCLUDING THE SUMMIT LEVEL VISITOR CENTER, ENGINE HOUSE #6 EXHIBIT SHELTER, THE HISTORIC LEMON HOUSE, THE SKEW ARCH BRIDGE, PICNIC AREA AND SEVERAL HIKING TRAILS.

ADDRESS: 110 FEDERAL PARK RD, GALLITZIN, PA 16641, UNITED STATES

PASSPORT STAMPS:

NOTES :

Black Moshannon State Park

VISTED DATE :   SPRING ◯ SUMMER ◯ FALL ◯ WINTER ◯

WEATHER : ☀️◯ ☁️◯ 🌧️◯ ❄️◯ ⛈️◯ 🌬️◯   🌡️TEMP :

FEE(S) :   RATING : ☆ ☆ ☆ ☆ ☆   WILL I RETURN?   YES / NO

LODGING :   WHO I WENT WITH :

DESCRIPTION / THINGS TO DO :

PERCHED HIGH ON THE ALLEGHENY PLATEAU, BLACK MOSHANNON STATE PARK IS A 3,394-ACRE PARK THAT FEATURES LUSH FORESTS AND WETLANDS.

INCLUDING THE FAMOUS BLACK MOSHANNON BOG NATURAL AREA.

SURROUNDED BY THE VAST MOSHANNON STATE FOREST, THE PARK CONSERVES UNIQUE, NATURAL ENVIRONMENTS AND IS HOME TO A DIVERSE ARRAY OF FAUNA AND FLORA, PROVIDING EXCELLENT BIRD AND WILDLIFE WATCHING FOR NATURE LOVERS.

RECREATIONAL ACTIVITIES IN THE PARK INCLUDE HIKING, MOUNTAIN BIKING, BOATING, CANOEING, FISHING, AND SWIMMING IN THE 250-ACRE BLACK MOSHANNON LAKE, WHICH IS FED BY SMALL STREAMS AND CLEAR SPRINGS.

CAMPING IS AVAILABLE IN THE PARK WITH BASIC CAMPSITES AND RUSTIC SELF-CATERING OVERNIGHT CABINS.

ADDRESS: 4216 BEAVER RD, PHILIPSBURG, PA 16866, UNITED STATES

PASSPORT STAMPS:

NOTES :

Caledonia State Park

VISTED DATE :   SPRING ○   SUMMER ○   FALL ○   WINTER ○

WEATHER :   ☀○   ⛅○   🌧○   ❄○   ⛈○   💨○   🌡TEMP :

FEE(S) :   RATING : ☆ ☆ ☆ ☆ ☆   WILL I RETURN?   YES / NO

LODGING :   WHO I WENT WITH :

DESCRIPTION / THINGS TO DO :

CALEDONIA STATE PARK IS A 1,125-ACRE STATE PARK THAT SPANS THE ADAMS AND FRANKLIN COUNTIES IS IN THE NORTHERNMOST SECTION OF THE BLUE RIDGE MOUNTAINS KNOWN LOCALLY AS SOUTH MOUNTAIN.

THE SOUTHERN PENNSYLVANIAN PARK IS NAMED AFTER THE CALEDONIA FURNACE, AN OLD IRON FURNACE THAT OPERATED IN 1837 AND FEATURES BEAUTIFUL NATURAL SCENERY OF LOW, ROLLING, FERTILE VALLEYS AND RUGGED QUARTZITE MOUNTAINS.

THE PARK HAS A RANGE OF RECREATIONAL FACILITIES, INCLUDING SELF-CATERING CAMPING CABINS AND BASIC CAMPSITES AND AN 18-HOLE, PAR 68, PUBLIC GOLF COURSE.

OTHER ACTIVITIES THAT CAN BE ENJOYED IN THE PARK INCLUDE HIKING, MOUNTAIN BIKING, AND WILDLIFE WATCHING.

ADDRESS: 101 PINE GROVE RD, FAYETTEVILLE, PA 17222, UNITED STATES

PASSPORT STAMPS:

NOTES :

Codorus State Park

VISTED DATE :   SPRING ◯   SUMMER ◯   FALL ◯   WINTER ◯

WEATHER :   ☀️◯   ⛅◯   🌧️◯   🌨️◯   ⛈️◯   💨◯   🌡️TEMP :

FEE(S) :   RATING : ☆ ☆ ☆ ☆ ☆   WILL I RETURN?   YES / NO

LODGING :   WHO I WENT WITH :

DESCRIPTION / THINGS TO DO :

CODORUS STATE PARK IS A 3,490-ACRE PARK IN THE ROLLING HILLS OF SOUTHERN YORK COUNTY THAT IS HOME TO THE 1,275-ACRE LAKE MARBURG AND SPECTACULAR NATURAL LANDSCAPES.

THE LAKE'S 26 MILES OF SHORELINE ATTRACTS A WEALTH OF MIGRATING WATERFOWL AND SHOREBIRDS THAT USE THE LAKE AS A REST STOP.

RECREATIONAL ACTIVITIES IN THE PARK AND ON THE LAKE INCLUDE LEISURE BOATING, CANOEING, AND KAYAKING, WARM WATER FISHING, SWIMMING, PICNICKING, HIKING AND MOUNTAIN BIKING.

SERVICES AND AMENITIES IN THE PARK INCLUDE AN AMPHITHEATER, BOAT LAUNCHING, AND MOORING SITES, CAMPING, MODERN RESTROOMS, AND AN ARRAY OF ENVIRONMENTAL EDUCATION PROGRAMS THAT ARE HOSTED THROUGHOUT THE YEAR.

ADDRESS: 2600 SMITH STATION ROAD, HANOVER PA 17331, UNITED STATES

PASSPORT STAMPS :

NOTES :

Delaware Water Gap National Recreation Area

VISTED DATE :   SPRING ○ SUMMER ○ FALL ○ WINTER ○

WEATHER : ☀️○ ⛅○ 🌧️○ 🌨️○ ⛈️○ 🌬️○   🌡️ TEMP :

FEE(S) :   RATING : ☆ ☆ ☆ ☆ ☆   WILL I RETURN? YES / NO

LODGING :   WHO I WENT WITH :

DESCRIPTION / THINGS TO DO :

THE DELAWARE WATER GAP NATIONAL RECREATION AREA IS A LARGE PARK IN THE POCONO MOUNTAINS ON THE BORDER OF NEW JERSEY AND PENNSYLVANIA WHICH IS HOME TO THE APPALACHIAN TRAIL, ALONG WITH MORE THAN 100 MILES OF HIKING TRAILS.

BOASTING INCREDIBLE NATURAL SCENERY ALONG THE BANKS OF DELAWARE RIVER, THE AREA FEATURES STEEP RIDGES AND DENSE HEMLOCK FORESTS, QUAINT HISTORIC COLONIAL VILLAGES AND AN ABUNDANCE OF DIVERSE FAUNA AND FLORA, AS WELL AS THE AREA'S NAMESAKE, THE SPECTACULAR 1000-FOOT-DEEP VALLEY BETWEEN THE MOUNTAIN RIDGES KNOWN AS THE 'WATER GAP.'

ADDRESS: 1978 RIVER ROAD, BUSHKILL, PENNSYLVANIA, UNITED STATES

PASSPORT STAMPS:

NOTES :

French Creek State Park

VISTED DATE :   SPRING ◯ SUMMER ◯ FALL ◯ WINTER ◯

WEATHER : ☀️◯ ⛅◯ 🌧️◯ 🌨️◯ ⛈️◯ 🌬️◯   🌡️TEMP :

FEE(S) :   RATING : ☆ ☆ ☆ ☆ ☆   WILL I RETURN? YES / NO

LODGING :   WHO I WENT WITH :

DESCRIPTION / THINGS TO DO :

FRENCH CREEK STATE PARK IS A 7,526-ACRE STATE PARK THAT STRADDLES THE BERKS AND CHESTER COUNTIES ALONG THE BANKS OF THE FRENCH CREEK.

LOCATED IN THE HOPEWELL BIG WOODS, THE PARK IS HOME TO TWO BEAUTIFUL LAKES, NAMELY THE 68-ACRE WARM WATER HOPEWELL LAKE AND THE 22-ACRE COLD WATER SCOTTS RUN LAKE, WHICH IS AN EXCELLENT FISHING LAKE.

THE PARK ALSO FEATURES VAST FORESTS, THE HOPEWELL FURNACE NATIONAL HISTORIC SITE, WHICH BOASTS A BEAUTIFULLY RESTORED COLD BLAST FURNACE DATING BACK TO THE 1830S, AND OVER 40 MILES OF HIKING, MOUNTAIN BIKING, AND EQUESTRIAN TRAILS.

VISITORS CAN ENJOY THE SIX PENNY DAY USE AREA AND GROUP CAMP, WHICH ARE LISTED ON THE NATIONAL REGISTER OF HISTORIC PLACES.

ADDRESS: 843 PARK RD, ELVERSON, PA 19520, UNITED STATES

PASSPORT STAMPS:

NOTES :

Friendship Hill Historic Site

VISTED DATE :   SPRING ◯   SUMMER ◯   FALL ◯   WINTER ◯

WEATHER :   ☀️◯   ⛅◯   🌧️◯   🌨️◯   ⛈️◯   🌬️◯   🌡️TEMP :

FEE(S) :   RATING : ☆ ☆ ☆ ☆ ☆   WILL I RETURN?   YES / NO

LODGING :   WHO I WENT WITH :

DESCRIPTION / THINGS TO DO :

FRIENDSHIP HILL HISTORIC SITE PRESERVES AND HONORS THE COUNTRY ESTATE AND HOME OF EARLY AMERICAN POLITICIAN AND STATESMAN ALBERT GALLATIN, A SWISS IMMIGRANT WHO SERVED HIS ADOPTED NATION DURING THE EARLY YEARS OF THE REPUBLIC.

GALLATIN IS RENOWNED FOR BEING SECRETARY OF THE TREASURY DURING THE JEFFERSON AND MADISON ADMINISTRATIONS AND FOR REDUCING THE NATIONAL DEBT, PURCHASING THE LOUISIANA TERRITORY AND FUNDING THE LEWIS & CLARK EXPLORATION DURING HIS 13-YEAR TENURE.

THE BEAUTIFULLY RESTORED FRIENDSHIP HILL HOUSE OFFERS VISITORS AN INTIMATE LOOK AT HIS LIFE DURING THIS TIME THROUGH INFORMATIVE DISPLAYS AND EXHIBITS.

TUCKED AWAY IN THE SOUTHWESTERN CORNER OF THE LAUREL HIGHLANDS, THE PRIVATE ESTATE IS OPEN TO VISITORS DAILY FROM SUNRISE TO SUNSET, ALL YEAR.

ADDRESS: 223 NEW GENEVA ROAD, POINT MARION, PA 15474, UNITED STATES

PASSPORT STAMPS:

NOTES :

Gifford Pinchot State Park

VISTED DATE :   SPRING ○   SUMMER ○   FALL ○   WINTER ○

WEATHER :   ☀ ○   ⛅ ○   🌧 ○   🌨 ○   ⛈ ○   🌬 ○   🌡 TEMP :

FEE(S) :   RATING : ☆ ☆ ☆ ☆ ☆   WILL I RETURN?   YES / NO

LODGING :   WHO I WENT WITH :

DESCRIPTION / THINGS TO DO :

GIFFORD PINCHOT STATE PARK IS A 2,338-ACRE FULL-SERVICE PARK BETWEEN THE TOWNS OF ROSSVILLE AND LEWISBERRY IN NORTHERN YORK COUNTY THAT FEATURES BEAUTIFUL LANDSCAPES OF ROLLING FARMLANDS, DENSE WOODLANDS, AND THE 340-ACRE PINCHOT LAKE.

THE LAKE IS THE CENTRAL ATTRACTION OF THE PARK AND OFFERS A RANGE OF WATER-BASED ACTIVITIES SUCH AS BOATING, FISHING, CANOEING AND KAYAKING, AND SWIMMING.

OTHER ACTIVITIES IN THE PARK INCLUDE HIKING, MOUNTAIN BIKING, PICNICKING, AND DISC GOLFING IN THE SUMMER, AND ICE-BOATING AND FISHING, ICE SKATING, AND CROSS-COUNTRY SKIING IN THE WINTER.

GIFFORD PINCHOT STATE PARK HAS A CAMPGROUND WITH YURTS, COTTAGES, CABINS, AND BASIC CAMPSITES ALONG WITH FACILITIES SUCH AS RESTROOMS, A CHILDREN'S PLAYGROUND, A VOLLEYBALL COURT, AND HORSESHOE PITS.

THERE IS ALSO A DESIGNATED BOAT LAUNCH AND SWIMMING AREA FOR GUESTS.

ADDRESS: 2200 ROSSTOWN RD, LEWISBERRY, PA 17339, UNITED STATES

PASSPORT STAMPS:

NOTES :

Made in the USA
Monee, IL
26 May 2022

97049286R00059